'I warmly welcome this important and timely book. When the state becomes the parent of someone else's child it has both a legal and a moral responsibility to be a good parent. Children do not come into public care for trivial reasons. They bring with them the impact of their earlier experiences. Foster carers generously open their homes and families to care for a hitherto unknown child. It is a wonderful gift of practical love. This book sets out both the challenges and the achievements of their day-by-day work. The service they provide both to the children and to society is remarkable and must be acknowledged in every possible way. This book should be widely read.'

– *The Rt. Hon. the Lord Laming*

'The warmth and integrity that weaves between the intricacies of living in a fostering family is breath-taking. This beautiful quote will stay with me forever:
"Always make sure they have a blanket when they leave. Don't wash it, as it needs to have a familiar smell to help them settle. Even our 16-year old took a blanket with her."'

– *Dr.h.c Jenny Molloy, Author, Adviser and Trainer for Looked After Children, Care Leavers Patron for The British Association of Social Workers England*

'This is a great guide, packed full of information and insight about how best to navigate the world of fostering. Written by those with impressive expertise and experience, this book will introduce the reader to the practicalities and complexities of being a foster carer. Fostering can be a life-changing experience for a child in care and this book will help carers navigate that territory so they can provide the very best of support for children who need it most.'

– *Isabelle Trowler, Chief Social Worker for Children*

'*Welcome to Fostering* is an informative, step-by-step insight into the world of fostering, from initial enquiry all the way through to a youngster going to university. It's the book I wish I'd had when I was considering fostering and in my first few years. A remarkable mix of questions, answers, case studies and real life examples from foster carers, youngsters in care and even a mother who'd had her children removed. I'd recommend it to anyone involved with fostering – or even just thinking about it.'

– *Maxine Taylor, Foster carer*

WELCOME TO FOSTERING

of related interest

The Foster Parenting Manual
A Practical Guide to Creating a Loving, Safe and Stable Home
John DeGarmo
Foreword by Mary Perdue
ISBN 978 1 84905 956 5
eISBN 978 0 85700 795 7

WELCOME TO
FOSTERING

A Guide to Becoming and Being a Foster Carer

Edited by ANDY ELVIN
and MARTIN BARROW

Foreword by LORRAINE PASCALE

Jessica Kingsley *Publishers*
London and Philadelphia

Figure on p.25, *Providing a Secure Base*, is reproduced with kind permission of Gillian Schofield and Mary Beek, University of East Anglia, Norwich, UK.

First published in 2017
by Jessica Kingsley Publishers
73 Collier Street
London N1 9BE, UK
and
400 Market Street, Suite 400
Philadelphia, PA 19106, USA

www.jkp.com

Library of Congress Cataloging in Publication Data
A CIP catalog record for this book is available from the Library of Congress

British Library Cataloguing in Publication Data
A CIP catalogue record for this book is available from the British Library

ISBN 978 1 78592 204 6
eISBN 978 1 78450 480 9

Printed and bound in the United States

Thanks to all the TACT staff, foster carers and
young people who contributed to this book

Contents

Foreword

Lorraine Pascale

I have been fortunate enough in my life to have had successful careers, firstly as a model and then as a chef and TV Presenter. My success is based not only on hard work, but also on my background, my experiences and how I was brought up. I am someone who has been fostered, and I have succeeded because of being in foster care, not in spite of it.

I know only too well the issues faced by children in care, and how good fostering can positively transform young lives. Far too often, media coverage about children in care focuses on the negative. I know from my own experience, and through being the Government Fostering Ambassador, that positive stories of children in foster care are plentiful, but rarely reported.

The truth is that foster families are not only important through childhood but remain important throughout life. I am still very much in touch with my foster family and I know that this is common.

It is important that the immense value and positive impact of foster care is recognised, and that more ordinary people consider doing something extraordinary for vulnerable children and young people, and that is to become foster carers.

This book offers real-life accounts by foster carers and young people in care, as well as expert advice and case studies. What I am most pleased about is how positive it is, and how it reflects the hopes and aspirations of so many children in foster care and their foster carers. It also highlights what I know from my own life to be true, that good fostering can build brighter, happier futures for children and young people.

So please enjoy this book. I hope it will make you think about what you might have to offer to children and young people in need of safe and stable homes. Remember that fostering is transformative for both the child and adult.

Unorthodox Beginnings

—— Solomon OB ——

A poem by TACT Ambassador Solomon OB about his
foster family:

> She graces stages
> West End bound, best friend found in a sibling who
>   chauffeured her halfway to crazy when we were younger
> My sister
>
> She called me baby
> As soon as I arrived through those airport doors, she
>   came charging, screaming, she hugged me with a force
>   you would expect from a lady who had not seen me
>   since 10 years before
> My mother
>
> He held down swaying relationships at home, light
>   anchors gripped to sea beds
> He sped from Brighton to Bristol and back via London
> Picked me up when I was man down behind the enemy
>   lines of my mind
> Before I self-destructed
> My brother
>
> He sits across Christmas dinner tables from me and I
>   wear his family name with pride

And with rose red eyes he told me:
'I love your mother now more than the day we got
    married'
50 years together a testament to the strength they're both
    possessing
My foster mother
My foster father

And yes, he calls my foster mother my mother but with
    no intent to disrespect my mother
I mean what else would you call your lover?
The woman who raised these kids, bathed these kids,
    takes them in like her own
Told them everything will be OK, told them they could be
    anything they wanted to be one day

What would you call her?
Saint? angel? magician for making ends meet when others
    may not have been able?
Many names from which to choose but I guess on this
    occasion mother will do
So yes we are fostered
And when I say this the lines on people's faces crumble up
    like discarded pages of paper laden with mistakes
But we are not mistakes on pages
We are simply awesome novels
With unorthodox beginnings

We are not mistakes on pages
We are simply a crooked introduction straightened out by
    proofreaders Pat and Vic
Whose love and guidance set the foundations for straight
    lines for us to write the rest of our story on
No we are not mistakes on pages
So this Christmas past I took your last name as a present
    to you to show you now that I can give and take

Victor Roy, Patricia Anne Brooker
I love you.

INTRODUCTION

—— Andy Elvin ——

Foster care, in the sense of people taking on children who are not their own and looking after them and bringing them up, has probably been around for as long as there has been society in the UK. Literature is full of examples of children being brought up by adults other than their parents. However, it was not until 1926 that the first formal laws covering fostering were passed in the UK. Since then, a number of laws have been passed governing foster care, and this is now the placement choice for the overwhelming majority of children who come into state care. There were 70,440 looked after children at 31 March 2016, an increase of 1% compared to 31 March 2015 and an increase of 5% compared to 2012. In 2016 the number of children in foster care continued to rise; of the 70,440 looked after children at 31 March 2016, 51,850 (74%) were cared for in foster placements – the same proportion as last year.

Foster care is vital, and our need for foster carers has never been greater. Lord Laming[1] recently described foster carers as 'Heroes of the State', and he is absolutely right about this. Day in day out, week in week out and year in year out, an army of altruistic, selfless and dedicated foster carers look after children who are among the most vulnerable in the UK – and who are full of amazing and sometimes limitless potential.

---

1   Lord Laming is a cross bench Peer with a long and distinguished career in Children's Social Care. He was Chief Inspector of the Social Services Inspectorate and led the Inquiry into the death of Victoria Climbié.

Fostering isn't easy; it's not for everyone, and if you choose to be a foster carer you will learn a great deal about the lives that some families lead and you will also learn a great deal about yourself. Fostering demands patience, empathy, creativity and above all compassion, and also a desire to help children recover from trauma and neglect and grow up to fulfil their potential.

The purpose of this book is to explain what fostering is, how to become a foster carer and what fostering is really like. It is packed with case studies from actual foster carers detailing their experience of becoming foster carers, the first placements, challenges they have faced along the way, what it has meant to them and the difference that they have been able to make. There are also case studies and quotes from children in foster care.

I hope that reading this book will encourage you to think seriously about foster care. Deciding to become a foster carer is, in part, an emotional decision, but it must also be a decision made with a clear understanding of what you are committing to. It is no less than the opportunity to transform a child's life. Good foster care and good foster carers are one of the most valuable resources the UK has. Very few other roles allow you to make such a positive impact on the lives of others.

The decision to put yourself forward as a foster carer may be the most important decision you ever make, both for you and for the children you are going to look after.

Chapter 1

SO YOU WANT TO BE A FOSTER CARER?

—— Bev Pickering ——

This chapter will discuss how to become a foster carer, and what the motivations might be, and it will raise some of the issues you need to think about when making this life-changing decision.

The decision to foster – the first step

Looking after children and young people who cannot be with their birth families is a difficult, challenging, complex and yet very rewarding thing to do.

An experienced foster carer recently said that if you are considering becoming a foster carer, 'You have to be a teacher, a carer, a friend, a psychologist, a social worker, a punch bag, a moral compass, have a sense of humour, be a bit mad and have lots of energy. You have to be resilient and enjoy children.'

There is a lot of truth in this, but other carers may describe key attributes and tasks very differently. And that's okay, because in reality no two foster carers are the same.

There is no such thing as the ideal applicant. Children and young people have different needs, and finding the right match is important. Having a choice of potential placements means better matches and increased likelihood of placement longevity. Foster carers can be single, co-habiting or married and be in heterosexual or same-sex relationships.

There are no restrictions on age, gender, disability, children in the household or childlessness, and each applicant is considered individually on what they can bring to fostering.

Perhaps the most important factor to be taken into consideration is the motivation to foster. Mistaken or unclear motivation can mean that carers are unprepared for the challenges of fostering. This in turn impacts on the child placed, often meaning another placement move for the child, which is what we need to avoid. The best reasons are those that do not involve intense personal needs and instead are child focused.

What motivates people to foster? The right reasons versus the wrong reasons

When someone enquires with the right motivation, the first conversation with people considering being a foster carer can be enlightening, humorous, heart-warming, emotional and satisfying. They may be at different stages of their journey – some are just asking questions, others are ready to apply – but they all have in common a passion for looking after children and a desire to help a child belong, achieve and be happy.

Some people share their life experiences and it is apparent that they have managed some very difficult personal challenges. Their resilience is evident and provides a strong place to start the journey to foster.

Some people tell us apologetically that they have 'just been a parent' and are not sure this is enough. It's a good starting place, and talking to their children can be insightful.

Some people have worked in other professions looking after children and want to transfer these skills to fostering. Again, this is a great starting place.

Other people have no childcare experience, but have life experience that has moulded them into caring, compassionate individuals with maturity and a positive can-do attitude.

We talk about the fostering process being a journey because there is no comparison with any other role. Let there not be any misconceptions: looking after other people's children, when the children may have experienced trauma, abuse, separation, rejection or anxiety, is hard work, and fostering agencies or the local authority have an important role in supporting the carers.

Some great quotes from applicants motivated for the right reasons include:

'I used to work in a special needs school and looked after many children who were in care. This inspired me to look at fostering as I just wanted to take the children home and care for them and give them the things they had never had in life – not just material objects but also a family and the security and stability they didn't have at home.'

'Seeing the children from Syria on the news inspired me to enquire about fostering – it's horrible to see so many refugee children without parents or families. I wanted to be able to help.'

'My children are all grown up and I think I did a good job. I'm proud of them and what they are doing with their lives. I could do that again for another child who needs love and guidance. I would give them [a looked-after child] what I gave my own: a family.'

'I'm young enough that teenagers will relate to me. They won't be able to "pull the wool over my eyes" because it's not so long ago that I was doing what they're doing. Young people need love, boundaries and consistency. They need to be accepted. They will kick against all that you try and do for them, but I will still be there!'

Alternatively, the first conversation about motivation to foster with people considering being a foster carer for the wrong reasons can be frustrating, disappointing and disillusioning. It reinforces the importance of ensuring that some applicants do not progress to being able to care for looked-after children.

There are a number of reasons people give regularly that make them unsuitable. Some of the most common relate to being lonely, wanting playmates for their children, needing money and wanting a bigger house. A selection of reasons given for wanting to become foster carers include:

'My wife is bored, I have seen other people who were fostering and thought it would be company for her.'

'My daughter is an only child. I can't have more children so if I foster, then the child can make my daughter's life happier and she will have someone to play with.'

'I think I want to adopt, but want to "try before I buy", so I thought being a foster carer would be good practice to see if I like having a child around.'

'I think I can make more money being a foster carer than having a lodger.'

'I want a bigger house and the council will give me one if I am a foster carer, and you get more "hand-outs". That will help my family out. It's hard sometimes to pay the bills.'

'My five children all share a room and there's space for another one because one of the bunk beds is empty. One more won't make a difference. It's a really big room.'

Obviously none of the above went forward as foster carers!

It is a much more difficult conversation with people considering being a foster carer when their motivations are misguided or selfish or it is not the right time for them to embark on the journey.

Some people are screened out at the early stage of enquiry, and we aim to do this while recognising their value and skills in other areas of their life, but letting them know that fostering is unlikely to be right for them at this time.

No one has the right to foster. One of the most important points to remember is that foster carers are recruited so we can find families for children who need a loving, caring home. We do not find children for families. Fostering focuses on the needs of the children being of paramount importance. Of course, looking after families is important, and more can be found about this in a later chapter.

What are the initial requirements?

Foster carers come from a wide range of backgrounds, cultures and ethnic groups. The most important criteria for becoming a foster carer are an ability to listen and empathise, to provide a stable and loving home and to speak up for the children.

Some people do not make an enquiry to foster because they believe they will not be considered due to their circumstances. Each enquiry is assessed on merit. The person taking a fostering enquiry will collate a lot of information about the applicants, their family, previous partners, children or childlessness, space and availability. This helps them to make an informed decision about whether to proceed.

We know there are some common concerns when people are thinking about fostering. To dispel any myths, here are some of the most frequently asked questions.

FAQs

Is there an age limit for fostering?
There is no upper age limit for fostering, but carers need to be fit enough to care for the children. There is not a defined age at which carers can begin fostering, but it is important

that they have the life experience and maturity to cope with the responsibility.

Am I able to foster if I am working?

This is something that is assessed on an individual basis. Fostering is a demanding role, and it is essential that carers are able to be flexible to meet the needs of the children in placement. There are regular meetings and training courses to attend, activities to promote and contact with family to facilitate, and availability is key to a successful placement. The fostering role should always be seen as a priority over any other work commitments carers may have.

Can I foster if I have a criminal conviction?

Committing an offence in the past will not necessarily preclude someone from fostering, unless it is of a violent or sexual nature. It is best for an applicant to disclose offences right at the start of their enquiry; then they can be advised if it may be a problem. Applicants will not be judged on their past, but on their ability to provide a safe environment for children.

Will my spouse or partner have to be assessed?

Couples are assessed together. This is an important part of knowing the family so that the right child is matched to the family. If one person is leading the enquiry, it is important that the other partner is fully on board. Sometimes, when couples are living apart but a significant time is spent together, then this would still be classed as a joint application. It is important that couples have fully explored what fostering means and how committed they both are to it.

Can I foster if I have pets?
Many foster carers have pets and they can often help children to relax and settle into a new home. As part of the family, pets will be included in the fostering assessment. It is important to ensure that they are up to date on their vaccinations and they are not likely to pose a threat to any children in the family.

Can I foster if I smoke?
Smoking will not necessarily prevent someone from fostering; however, babies and young children will not be placed into a household where people smoke (even if this is outside). Agencies and local authorities have different rules about the age of children that can be placed with a smoker, but certainly it would not be a child younger than two and probably not under five. Even with older children, it is a requirement that there is no smoking in the home or the car.

Do I have to be able to drive?
This may depend on where an applicant lives. The main concern is that a carer will be able to get the children to school, to activities and to contact meetings, and attend meetings and training themselves. If they live in an urban area with good transport links, driving may not be essential.

Do I need to own my own home?
Applicants need a stable home for a foster child with no risk of eviction. As part of the assessment process references are sought from either the landlord if you rent, or the bank if you have a mortgage.

CASE STUDY

My husband and I realised early on that we couldn't have children, so we threw ourselves into our work and accepted that we would probably never be parents. But something was missing from our lives; we had love and time to share, so we decided we would like to foster children.

We approached TACT (The Adolescent and Children's Trust) as it was a not-for-profit organisation. The staff were incredibly positive and knowledgeable and very passionate about helping the children, and we therefore couldn't wait to start our journey to becoming foster carers.

While the amount of personal information about us required during the assessment process felt intrusive, we were as honest as we could be, as this would enhance our chances of being matched with children who were right for us. Our panel date came, and with the help of our social worker we breezed through it.

Soon after becoming TACT-approved foster carers we got our first placement – two bouncing boys under the age of three. We loved every minute of that placement, which made our house busy, noisy and happy. The difference in those boys in a short space of time was phenomenal, and we felt that along with the social worker and help from TACT we had given them a better chance in life and they were allowed back home to mum.

Then along came a little girl; again we saw a huge difference in her, and our first Christmas with a foster child in placement was a joy to behold. Once again, we had successfully done our duty, and she went back to mum.

During that placement we agreed to take on another child – J, a shy and withdrawn two-and-a-half-year-old girl, who didn't speak. We got down to providing the loving care that she needed, overcoming her food issues and speech problem, and alleviating her fear of being left alone. Every day came a new achievement – she was our little superstar. The plan for J was adoption, and it had never been our intention to adopt, as we wanted to help lots of children. But she was special, and we wanted her as much as she wanted us, so we asked if we could be considered. Once again, TACT were helpful and supportive and we began the adoption process.

During this time, Baby A – J's half sibling – was born. The plan was to put Baby A into foster care and then either return her to her mum or put her up for adoption. We wanted to foster Baby A, and then if the plan was to adopt we wanted to keep the children together. The local authority was not sure that the baby should be placed with us, as if the plan for Baby A was not adoption it might have a negative effect on both children. However, we were not convinced, and our support social worker persuaded the local authority to allow us to foster Baby A. We will be eternally grateful to TACT for that, as we eventually adopted Baby A.

Our family is now complete; we have two wonderful girls who are loved, and give so much love, and we will always be in debt to TACT for helping us to make that happen, not just for us, but our whole family – our parents are now grandparents; our siblings are now aunties and uncles.

Taking action

If someone is considering fostering, the best advice we can give is to pick up the phone, search online and gather all of the information you need. A good fostering service member of staff should assist the enquirer to consider what fostering entails, and not rush them through the process before they are ready.

To help a potential applicant, they should consider what skills and qualities they have. Do they match the diagram below?

What young people think (TACT young peoples survey)

If applicants think they have some (or even better, all) of these characteristics, a looked-after child may benefit from their care.

An interesting question for potential applicants to ask themselves is: 'What can I provide for children and young people?'

A popular and effective model in fostering is that of the 'secure base' which identifies the five elements of a secure base that looked-after children need. Considering these at the start of a fostering journey may help focus applicants on the task to be undertaken.

The Secure Base Model

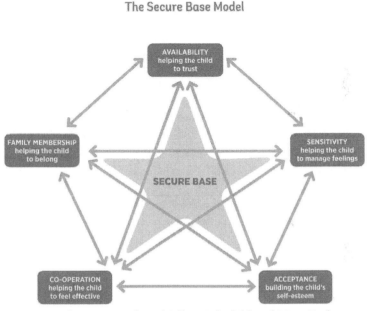

Providing a secure base (Gillian Schofield and Mary Beek, University of East Anglia, Norwich, UK)

CASE STUDY

Bob and I had planned for quite a while to become foster carers and purposely bought a bigger house. Soon after we had been cleared to foster we went from zero children to three, all siblings, which was a bit of a shock to the system. Our daily routines changed drastically, and there was an overwhelming sense of responsibility knowing that we had to look after these three little people. The first few weeks were hectic – meeting with the school, social workers, opticians, GPs, dentist and so on. Fortunately our families are very supportive and helped us immensely. We were also blessed with working alongside brilliant social workers both at our fostering agency and the local authority social services, who have all helped us so much.

We have four miniature schnauzers – Arthur, Betty, Margaret and Mary. At first the children were petrified of them, but now each has a favourite. The dogs have helped them to develop an element of responsibility, as they recognise when they need to be fed and cared for and often act on this.

Over the past year we have learned that children don't really want material things in life – they would much prefer having time spent with them. By offering them our time and attention they have been able to really blossom as individuals and their personalities have developed so much. We have also found that education isn't just gained in school. Holidays, meals in restaurants, trips to the park or even just visiting friends and family all enable the children to learn new things. Their confidence has developed dramatically through doing these things.

Bob and I absolutely love being foster carers. We both feel an immense sense of pride in being able to have such a positive impact on the lives of children who may have been through trauma. It is hard work, and at times we are faced with challenges; however, that is part and parcel of being a foster carer. The children have enriched our lives beyond recognition and we have learned so much over the past year. I would recommend becoming a foster carer to anybody.

Becoming a foster parent is one way that you can make a real and lasting impact on a child's life. A very apt motivational quote comes from Dr Forest E. Witcraft in *Within My Power*[1]:

> A hundred years from now
> it will not matter
> what my bank account was
> the sort of house I lived in
> or the kind of car I drove
> But the world may be different, because
> I was important in the life of a child.

Conclusion

Applying to become a foster carer is a big step and not one to be taken lightly. However, one of the most common mistakes people make is to rule themselves out based on the assumption that a local authority or fostering agency will not want them as a foster carer. Foster carers come from all backgrounds, in all kinds of family units, and are of all ages. Please check with your local authority or fostering agency, and don't rule yourself out, because by doing that you may be denying a vulnerable child a fantastic home with you. We look forward to hearing from you!

---

1   http://teachers-and-parents.blogspot.com/2008/02/within-my-power-by-dr-forest-e-witcraft.html

Chapter 2

BECOMING A
FOSTER CARER

—— Andy Elvin ——

So, you've read about it, you've talked about it, you've thought about it and decided to take the plunge. You think fostering is for you and you want to get started. This chapter explains the stages you will go through in order to become a foster carer and includes a case study where a current foster carer explains their journey from the decision to foster to their first placement.

The first thing to consider is whom you want to foster for. There are a number of different options. You can foster for your local authority – such authorities have long supported foster carers and have their own cohort of in-house foster carers. There are also independent fostering agencies, which are split into two main types:

- Charitable or not-for-profit fostering agencies, such as TACT, Action for Children or Barnardo's. These charities recruit, train and support foster carers and then local authorities enter contracts with the charities for the foster carers to look after vulnerable children. All the fees the charities receive providing these fostering placements go into supporting the foster carers, supporting the children directly or providing additional services that will benefit the child and their placement.

- Commercial fostering agencies. Some of these are very small scale and the owners also run and manage these agencies. However, there are increasing numbers of very large commercial fostering agencies, which tend to be owned by venture capital firms that view fostering as a business within which they can make a sizeable return on their investment. Because the fees for fostering are coming from local authorities, they view the income as being very secure, as local authorities will not go bankrupt. Though the foster carers who work for these large commercial agencies are usually great, as most foster carers generally are, there is no disguising the fact that some of the money in fees goes directly into the pockets of the venture capital owners.

It is worth considering the different types of agencies you can foster for and maybe talking to the different types of agencies about the support you would receive; if possible, try and talk to foster carers who already foster for these agencies as they can give you a good insight into the level of support, training and supervision that you will receive.

All children placed in foster care come through local authorities, so it is the local authorities that make the placement decision. Often, if you want to foster babies or young children, you may be better advised to approach your local authority and foster for them. Charitable fostering agencies tend to be asked to look after older children, sibling groups and specialist placements such as parent and child placements. Different sorts of foster caring are outlined below.

The different sorts of foster caring

Short-term foster care

This is for children and young people whose care plans are uncertain. The child may be placed with you following removal from the family home due to concerns, or due to the birth parent's unavailability because of illness. A child may require a placement following a breakdown in the arrangement with another foster carer or adopter.

Short-term placements could last for a few days, a few weeks or sometimes a number of years. The child may return home, move to live with other family members who have been assessed, or move into a long-term fostering or adoption placement. Short-term fostering can be extremely varied, and your agency will ensure that you are equipped to manage the challenges and complexities of this. Training and support will be available.

Many short-term placements made with foster carers move into long-term arrangements. This is as a result of the good initial matching process, and the subsequent hard work and commitment of the foster carers.

Long-term foster care

This is for children and young people who will not be returning to their birth family. Long-term care requires a commitment from the foster carer to provide care for as long as is needed. This may be up to the age of 18 years, and even beyond – under the new Staying Put arrangement designed to help young people move on to independence when they are ready.

Long-term foster care differs from adoption due to the child's legal care status. In long-term foster care the children and young people remain in the care of the local authority and fostering regulations apply throughout the time they are living with you. As a long-term foster carer you will not be granted parental responsibility for the child you are caring for.

Sometimes a child requires a long-term placement and a match is identified at the outset. In other cases, a child may be placed as a short-term placement and the care plan then becomes long term. If both the child and the foster carer want the arrangement to become long term, this will be considered by the child's social worker in consultation with the agency.

As a long-term foster carer you will get to see the young person in your care flourish into a young adult – the rewards gained from this are multiple. As their foster carer you will build a strong relationship with the young person as you guide them through their childhood and meet the challenges along the way.

Emergency foster care

Many short-term placements occur in an emergency. You will not have the opportunity to meet the child or young person beforehand and you have to be ready to accept the child when they arrive. Due to the nature of the emergency, the child may be brought to you by a duty social worker or the police. The child or young person will require additional reassurance and welcome from you.

A great deal of flexibility from foster carers is required, as once you have agreed to a placement the child will quickly be placed with you. Emergency fostering usually lasts for a few days while future plans for the child are made, although it can sometimes lead to a short-term or long-term placement.

Some carers agree to receive referrals for placements outside office hours, and these foster carers are asked if they are prepared to take a placement at any time of the day or night.

Foster care for children and young people with disabilities

As a disability carer, you'll be offering specialist care to children with complex needs, which can include physical disabilities, medical conditions or learning difficulties. Caring for a child with a disability can be hugely rewarding, as you give the child the opportunity to reach their full potential.

Becoming a disability foster carer can seem quite daunting, but you will be provided with training and guidance to ensure that you can give the child the support they need to thrive.

Sibling foster care

It is important for siblings to remain together where possible when they need a foster care placement. Children placed in foster care have said that this is what they want, although there may be occasions when siblings cannot be all placed together due to concerns about behaviour or safety.

Fostering sibling groups can sometimes be challenging and demanding, but it is also extremely rewarding. Foster carers who want to give brothers and sisters a stable family home, particularly those who can care for the larger sibling groups, are very much sought after. It is a requirement that only same-sex siblings can share bedrooms.

Short-break foster care

This is when you provide care for a child or young person over a short period of time, usually somewhere between a weekend and a fortnight. Short-break foster care gives families and foster carers a network of support when they most need it.

As a short-break carer you will join your local network of carers to support each other with respite care when required. Looking after a family and fostering is a demanding role, so when things do get tough and carers need time away, you can be there to provide that much-needed support.

Parent and child foster care

All children need a loving and safe home, and if it is possible that a child can remain with their parents, this is a positive outcome. Child and parent fostering is where you offer a home to one or maybe both parents and the child. The parent may be under 18 and will be a looked-after child themselves. Sometimes they will be placed during the pregnancy so that you can help them prepare.

There are a number of reasons why a parent may require a placement. They may need additional support, help and advice, and your role will be to teach and support them so that they can move to independence. Or there may be significant concerns about parenting capacity and assessments are being made about their ability to provide care to their child. In this situation as a foster carer, you will be contributing to the assessments and maintaining clear and concise recordings to provide to the social worker and the court.

Child and parent foster carers are provided with specialist training and require additional approval by the fostering panel.

Step-down foster care (also known as residential to fostering)

Sometimes a child or young person needs the type of environment that only residential children's homes can provide. However, as they receive support and care to address the behaviours that caused them to be placed in the home, they improve to the point that they are considered ready to live in a family environment, and a foster carer is sought.

If you are interested in this type of fostering, there are opportunities to meet the child or young person, and introductions are set at an acceptable pace for the child to adjust. You receive additional support in the early stages from the residential unit, and there is a carefully put together care plan so that all professionals and supports are in place.

Step-down fostering helps children make the transition back into a family unit, which can deliver a much better outcome for them.

Remand fostering

This offers safe family accommodation for alleged young offenders from the age of 10 to 17, while they are awaiting trial or sentencing. Custody can be damaging for vulnerable young people, perpetuating a cycle of imprisonment and re-offending. Remand foster care offers young people the support needed to rethink their actions and to alter their behaviour.

Foster carers are sometimes nervous about taking on remand foster placements as they fear that the children and young people are much more complex. Your agency will assist you with the skills and knowledge that you may need for this type of foster care. Often, foster carers already experienced in working with teenagers can easily make this transition.

This type of care can especially suit people who may have worked with young offenders, including probation or youth justice workers, police and prison officers, youth workers or teachers.

Foster care for unaccompanied
asylum-seeking children

Many of these young people have been separated from their families, either in their homeland or during transit to the UK. As you might expect, these children are often extremely distressed and frightened as a result of the overwhelming experience they have been through. Fostering young people who are seeking asylum does come with its challenges but is also hugely rewarding as you start to see them settle into their new life in the UK. In some cases, the children will speak little or no English.

As a foster carer specialising in asylum-seeking fostering, you can help and teach these children the skills they need to successfully build a new life and ways to overcome their traumatic past. Your agency will work very close with you and provide specialist training to help you support these children.

Local authorities always try to place children and young people with families who may have some knowledge of their culture or language. However, this is not always possible, but foster carers who are resourceful will be able to facilitate the young person in maintaining links with their culture.

Staying Put

Staying Put is simply a new piece of legislation that allows children in foster care in England to stay with their foster family until they are 21 years old. This addresses a key area of discrimination against children in care which meant that they, unlike children with their birth families, could not stay in their home after the age of 18. There is a difference in the fees and allowances that come with Staying Put, and your fostering agency will be able to discuss these with you. It is highly unlikely that you will begin your fostering career with a Staying Put placement, as they tend to happen with children you have been looking after for some years before they turn 18.

Whichever foster care option you choose, you will be a welcome addition to the foster care workforce. There are six stages in your journey to becoming a foster carer, and these are detailed below.

The six stages in your journey to becoming a foster carer

1 Initial enquiry

Making the first contact to say you are considering fostering can be a really big step, but there's nothing to worry about. The initial enquiry is an opportunity for you to find out more about fostering and the application process, to help you decide if it is something that you want to pursue.

At this stage you are not making any commitment – you will simply have an informal chat with an enquiries team, ask any questions that you have and answer a few basic questions about yourself and your motivation to become a foster carer. Some of these questions are entirely practical; for example, each foster child must be able to have their own separate bedroom, so you must physically have space in your home to offer to a foster child.

2 Home visit

The next step is for a supervising social worker to visit you at your home. The visit will involve a more detailed discussion about your circumstances, your family, any experience that is relevant to fostering and your motivations to become a foster carer.

The home visit is a finding-out session for everyone. The social worker will ask you about your understanding of fostering and the needs of looked-after children, and you will have the opportunity to ask further questions that you may have about the process and the effect that fostering might have on your lives. It is always a good idea to write down some questions you think you might want to ask or issues you think you might want to raise. There are no stupid questions in this process, and it is important to raise anything you're worried or concerned about at this initial-visit stage. If you go forward for assessment then you are entering a process where almost every aspect of your life – your current relationship, relationship history and your childhood – will be discussed. Many, many people from many, many different backgrounds and experiences become foster carers. Never assume that, because you may have had a difficult childhood or difficult adult relationships, this excludes you from becoming a foster carer. Some of the very best foster carers come from backgrounds that might be described as difficult. It is not where you have come from or the experiences that you have had that matter, it is your perspective on those experiences, what you have learned and what you have gained from them that is important in the process of becoming a foster carer.

If you are married or live with a partner, you both need to be equally committed to fostering. Your partner will need to be present at the home visit as they are classed as a secondary carer, and will need to be involved in the assessment process from this point onwards.

3 Introductory training

As a foster carer you should have access to an extensive training package, starting with the Skills to Foster course. This three-day introductory training course is designed to give you an insight into the role of a foster carer, the expectations of you and your family, and some of the other people that you will be required to work with, such as the child's family, their social worker and other professionals.

The course will be insightful and sometimes emotional as you explore some of the reasons that children come into care, the experiences that they may have had, and your role in helping to manage their behaviour and development.

You will also meet some existing foster carers, who will share their experience of the application process, getting their first placement and the support that they receive, and they will answer any questions you may have. You may also meet some children who have been in foster care and who will explain what fostering has been like from their perspective and what it means to them.

As the course is attended by other people who want to become foster carers, it is a shared experience, and you will learn from the motivations of others, as they will learn from you. Foster care is about relationships, the most important being the relationship between you and the children you foster. The relationship between you and professional networks is also very important. Some of the other potential foster carers you meet at the Skills to Foster course and those at subsequent training courses you go on may well turn out to be people who form an important part of your support network.

4 Application and assessment

'The assessment was like a really, really in-depth "This is Your Life".' (foster carer)

There is no underplaying the depth and intimacy of the assessment process. If you become a foster carer you are going to be entrusted with the care of some of the UK's most vulnerable children. It is absolutely vital that foster carers who are approved have the necessary quality and insights to offer excellent care to these children.

After completing your application form you will be allocated a supervising social worker who will work with you to complete a detailed assessment of your suitability to become a foster carer – this is called a Form F assessment.

The assessment involves a number of checks, including medical, financial, police and background checks which are known as DBS in England and Wales and PVG in Scotland. These check whether police or local authorities have any concerns about you working with vulnerable children. And because fostering involves the whole family, checks will also be carried out on other members of the household. As part of the assessment process, contact is also made with other significant adults in your life, including ex-partners and adult children – your social worker will explain in more detail what the checks entail and who needs to be involved.

Alongside the checks, you will have regular meetings with your social worker for detailed discussions on a range of subjects relevant to your suitability to become a foster carer. You may find some of these conversations uncomfortable or intrusive, although many potential foster carers actually find them refreshing and empowering. There are not many times in our lives when we are encouraged to reflect in such depth on the forces that have made us who we are as adults. You will find yourself returning to events and issues you do not think about very often or haven't thought about since they happened. This can be a pleasant experience but sometimes it can be difficult and it is important to look after yourself during the assessment process. Always say to the social worker if you are struggling with the topic and would like some time to reflect and come back to it.

By the end of the assessment your assessing social worker should be able to win 'Mastermind' with you as their specialist subject.

5 Approval

The final stage of the application process is the panel review. A fostering panel consists of a group of experienced, independent care professionals who will review your assessment and make a recommendation to the agency about your suitability as a foster carer. All of the information gathered during your assessment is compiled into a single report, which is presented to the fostering panel.

Carers can often get very anxious at this stage, but there is really no need to worry. You will meet with your social worker on a regular basis throughout your assessment and they will raise any concerns that they have well in advance of you going before the panel. It can be a very celebratory and joyous occasion, as it marks your passage from the assessment to becoming a registered and approved foster carer. Many new foster carers like to make a day of it and go out and have a meal or do something to celebrate their achievement.

6 Your first placement

Your journey doesn't end with approval – it's just the start! As soon as you are approved, your agency will begin the process of matching you to your first placement and will continue to support you through every step of your fostering career.

CASE STUDY

Assessment and approval process

Both the assessment and approval process were reassuringly robust. I had to fit meetings and training around a full-time job, and the social worker I was working with lived some distance from me. So from start to finish the whole process took 15 months. Honestly I felt quite out on my own at times. I didn't know any other foster carers and I had no point of reference as to how things were going. As a result, I did seek reassurance from the agency I was applying through, and they put me in contact with foster carers who were in a similar situation to me. For example, I am a single foster carer, and the social worker I was dealing with raised concerns about aspects of this but couldn't advise on how perceived difficulties could be tackled. A quick chat with an experienced single foster carer from my agency was more than reassuring and it taught me that reaching out to others in the fostering community was a coping mechanism I could rely on.

The process tests you. But through it you also get the opportunity to evaluate yourself and how much you really want to be a foster carer. This self-analysis will serve you well in the future, as you will always need to consider your own responses as well as those of the children you are looking after. Fostering brings many emotional reactions to the surface. You wouldn't be human if it didn't, but the most important thing is to be able to recognise that, reflect and then respond appropriately. The initial stages of assessment and approval are an introduction to that, and as I have continued on my fostering journey I am trying to build on those skills and am always looking for further ways to build my resilience and understanding of trauma.

Motivations for becoming a foster carer

I had thought about fostering for many years and had done a lot of research and soul searching about what I could offer. My own situation has meant that I have been involved in the care of my disabled sister since she became gravely ill in our teenage years. During times when she was exceptionally ill I didn't live at home with my family. I wasn't in the care system as I was fortunate to have an extended family and good friends who looked after me when my parents couldn't. But what I recall from that time was that I felt supported and cared for. Had that experience not been so positive, things could have been very different for me in terms of my personal development and focus on education. As I moved through life I felt very lucky to have had that loving experience during such difficult times and it made me truly realise the value of consistent and empathetic care.

It's not possible for me to truly understand how traumatising it is for any child not to be raised by their biological family. But all of my life experiences have given me a good level of emotional understanding, patience and resilience. These were the qualities that I felt could help me as a foster carer. Equally I felt I had a lot to offer, and I was excited about the prospect of giving stability and warmth to young people when they needed it most.

Having taught for some years and also volunteered on various children's projects at my local community centre, I realised that I could be calm and kind when it was needed most, and I enjoyed being a part of a young person's development. Despite not having children myself I have always loved spending time with them, and I was very keen to make that my focus in life. After 17 years in educational publishing and teaching I was offered redundancy, which gave me the opportunity to take stock and pursue my other ambition to care for others. I had space in my home and felt I had a good life that I could share with children who were not able to be in the care of their families.

What the initial visit was like

Any nerves I had about the initial visit were eased by the thorough and reassuringly relaxed approach of the social worker from my fostering agency. We talked through my personal circumstances, family background and motivations for wanting to be a foster carer.

Many of the questions and scenarios I was asked to consider seemed straightforward, but there were more probing and deeply personal aspects that I was asked to divulge. My instinct was to be completely open, and I laid bare all the areas of myself and my life experiences. This felt right, and although I was worried that events I have experienced might be viewed negatively, I learned that this was part of my own emotional make-up. It had not only informed my decision to be a foster carer but had also added to my capacity to be empathetic and my ability to understand the effects of trauma.

On leaving, the social worker asked for various forms of ID and requested a look around the house. I had expected this but was taken aback when I was asked if I had any weapons on the premises. As it happened there was only a boomerang picked up on a backpacking trip; this was a lighter moment, but it did also remind me that I would always be under scrutiny and I had to learn to expect the unexpected from now on.

The assessment process – what it entailed and what it felt like

After the initial visit from the social worker I attended the three-day Skills to Foster course. It was good to be in a room with people who also wanted to be a foster carer, and we all began to comprehend the full extent of what we would be taking on. Nothing was sugarcoated, and we were tested on our responses and instincts about certain case studies and scenarios. It was led by a social worker from the agency and an experienced foster carer. I remember taking in the procedural elements from the former and absorbing the personal experiences and obvious dedication to fostering from the latter. Each day felt like a lot of information and gave me much to consider on a personal level, but I remained enthusiastic about fostering and wanted to learn more.

Not long after the course I was informed that I was being progressed and assigned an external social worker to take me through the approval process. I was visited at home again and realised that all the meetings would likely take two to three hours. Each time was encouraging but also emotionally draining, as we went through all the impactful events of my life, family relations both positive and negative, past relationships, support network, personal successes and disappointments. There was a lot of paperwork – also a useful introduction to that element of fostering – and face-to-face meetings were requested with my family, friends and previous long-term partner.

It could feel like a very intrusive process, and in fact many friends and family members commented on that, especially those who were spoken to about my suitability for fostering. I suspect that is because they know me, they know my intentions and my character, but I understood that I would be taking responsibility for some very vulnerable children, so I didn't feel it was misplaced, and I felt reassured by how serious an undertaking the assessment process was. Your ability to cope with difficulties, tension and openness are an essential indication of how you will deal with fostering going forward – so it made sense that this was part of the assessment process.

The panel – what it entailed, what it felt like in practical terms and the emotional impact

Despite knowing that by this late stage in the process it is unlikely you won't be approved, I found the panel daunting, in that I was faced by a number of professionals on my own. The external social worker I had been assigned did join me; she had come a good distance to do so and was not entirely happy about this. She made me aware of her displeasure before we went into the meeting room and it wasn't the best start, but at this point I didn't want anything to ruin my chance to present myself well. I went in feeling focused and ready, and for the most part the panel were very positive and reassuring.

One issue raised was the area where I lived, which was felt to be a point of concern. This was a surprise to me as it hadn't been mentioned previously. I was living on an estate with some private but also a good amount of social housing. It had its problems, but overall it was a town with a thriving economy, so the pockets of disadvantage had never felt that deep to me.

As I was active in the local community centre I was aware that there were families experiencing tough economic situations, but I also expressed that I was well informed and felt that every street in the UK had its problems. In my case I knew where and what they were in my neighbourhood, and I wasn't oblivious to hardship experienced in society.

Overall the panel experience was fine; it was brief and almost an anti-climax after so many months of expectation. My agency was delighted with the outcome and made me feel welcome as a new member of their team. I had not had the most positive experience with the social worker assigned to me for the assessment process, but almost two years on I have since worked with a number of excellent social workers and this has helped me realise that, as in all professions, there will always be some approaches or opinions that you might not share and you have to learn to get the best out of each working relationship. I see that as part of my responsibility to the child I am looking after.

Overall, and especially in relation to my own agency, I have felt massively supported and had a very positive experience with the social workers I have worked with.

On the day of the panel I especially recall that before I went in I sat in my car as I had arrived early. I was listening to Bradley Wiggins on 'Desert Island Discs' and he spoke about the relationship he didn't have with his father, how he had left him and his mother when Bradley was young, and how this impacted him all through his life, most notably after his great successes in the Tour de France and the Olympics. It struck me that not having the support of parents or parental figures in the early years of life continues to have an impact. We don't need the children we care for to be medal winners, but that's not to say that they can't be. Being caring and supportive may just keep them on a safe path or it may be the start of a new and positive direction for them. Either way, whatever the outcome, I knew I wanted to invest myself in that and I felt positive about my future in fostering.

Conclusion

The assessment process to become a foster carer is a very in-depth and thorough piece of work. It may appear daunting, but many foster families actually enjoy the opportunity to talk about themselves and their lives and to review the experiences that have brought them to the point of wanting to be a foster carer. As a foster carer you are going to be looking after some of the most vulnerable children in the UK, so it is important that you are sure and that your agency is sure that fostering is right for you.

Chapter **3**

HOW DO CHILDREN BECOME FOSTERED?
—— Andy Elvin and Louise Cox ——

There are a variety of ways in which children become looked after in the care system. This chapter will explain the main routes by which children come into care and some of the legal and statutory processes that lead to your foster children arriving with you.

The overwhelming majority of children come into care because of concerns about their safety and welfare within their family home.

Some children come into care through a voluntary agreement. This agreement comes under Section 20 of the 1989 Children Act, which allows birth parents to agree that their child comes into care for a period of time. This may be for reasons that have nothing whatsoever to do with poor parenting or concerns about the child's safety, for example if one parent is admitted to hospital and there is only one parent and no extended family who can look after the child. It can also happen in instances of poor mental health where the parent may be voluntarily or involuntarily detained for a period of time under the Mental Health Act and there are no other options for the care of the child. It is more likely under Section 20 that the child comes into care because there are some concerns but the parents are co-operating fully and are content that the child comes into care or certain issues are addressed. A typical example of this may be a parent who has a substance misuse issue –

most commonly alcohol – and the child comes into care while the parent undergoes a period of in- or outpatient rehabilitation. Under Section 20, the expectation is that the child will be reunited with the birth parent in the short to medium term.

Section 20 should not be used if the parent does not consent to the child coming into care or if it is likely that the child will remain in care long term and the parent is unlikely to consent to this.

The majority of children come into care when the local authority takes out a court order to give them a share of parental responsibility and the child is removed from the family home, not necessarily with the parents' consent, because of concerns about the child's well-being or welfare. Social workers cannot remove children from the family home without the consent of the courts. The only professionals who can remove the child without the permission of the courts are the police. The police have powers of protection that allow them to remove the child for up to 72 hours from the family home if they think there is an immediate danger of significant harm to the child were they to leave them in there. This typically happens outside regular office hours when the police cannot call on the assistance social workers and judge that the child will suffer significant harm if they do not take action (often as a result of parental intoxication, domestic violence or criminality). In order for a social worker to remove the child from the family home they have to apply for an order under the 1989 Children Act in the family court.

There are a number of orders that the local authority can apply for. If it is an emergency and the child needs to be removed, then they may apply for an emergency protection order, giving the local authority parental responsibility for seven days and allowing them to remove the child to a place of safety, often a foster home. However, the local authority still has to go back to court for a more long-lasting order.

Often it is not an emergency and therefore the local authority will issue care proceedings and apply for an interim care order, giving the local authority legal parental responsibility for a month. This may be renewed numerous times as long as the case remains in care proceedings in the family courts, which involve the local authority seeking to remove the child from the family permanently. The expectation of the family courts is that these cases go on no longer than 26 weeks. Most of the 26 weeks is taken up by the gathering of evidence, assessments and statements from the various parties before a final hearing (which typically lasts between two days and a week) when all the evidence is heard and then a judge makes a decision as to whether the child will be permanently removed from the family home. In these cases, parents are fully legally represented and they receive legal aid. The local authority is represented through a solicitor, and the child is represented by the Child and Family Court Advisory and Support Service (Cafcass). The role of the Cafcass officer is to represent the voice of the child in the family court. Cafcass is part of the Ministry of Justice and made up largely of social workers and lawyers whose role it is to represent children in family court proceedings and some other legal proceedings.

Children often come into foster care at the start of this process, and therefore you may find yourself looking after a child who is subject to care proceedings. If this is the case, there may be quite a high level of contact with the birth family during the care proceedings. This is very important as the local authority is not allowed to pre-judge the outcome of the care proceedings and is committed to maintaining a good relationship between the child and the family and making sure that the bonds between them are not broken during the process. This is because one of the possible outcomes may be to return the child to the family home. Contact can be a very positive experience for the child, and the foster carer must try to promote and facilitate full contact. However, managing extensive family contact can be challenging for foster carers if the contact is of a very poor quality. If this is the case, and you think it is having a detrimental effect on the child, you must mention this to your supervising social worker and to the child social worker. Although it is important that the contact is maintained, the welfare of the child is paramount, and if the contact is damaging the child to the extent that they are experiencing significant harm, it is important that the court knows about this and takes a view about the level of contact.

As a foster carer you may also be asked for your views as part of the care proceedings. Sadly, the family courts far too seldom hear from the people who know most about the child – those who are looking after them on a daily basis. If you feel that you have information that you think is important for the court to hear, then please share this with your supervising social worker. Never be afraid to advocate for your child. If you feel that the plan that is being presented to court is not right for the child you are looking after, then you must say something. You can speak to your social worker, to the child social worker, to the independent reviewing officer or to the Cafcass officer. When advocating for the child, always be reasonable and measured, but do not ever feel that your opinion is worthless because you are not one of the titled professionals or an officer of the court. You will know more about what kind of family environment will suit your foster child than anyone else in the professional network. You are the expert on your foster child, and your view should be listened to, respected and discussed.

There are several possible outcomes at the end of care proceedings. The child will generally either be returned to the birth parents, placed with relatives, placed in foster care or placed for adoption. If the child is removed permanently from the birth family, it may be that staying with you as a long-term fostering arrangement will be the long-term care plan for the child. There are a number of possible outcomes at the end of care proceedings in terms of placement, and one of them is long-term foster care. Another possibility is adoption. Younger children, particularly those under five, are far more likely to go forward for adoption. An increasing number of children are moving to live with extended family members under special guardianship orders. A special guardianship order is like an adoption order but does not completely extinguish the birth parents' parental responsibility. There is more about special guardianship orders, which are also open to foster carers to take out, later in this book.

If the plan is that the child lives long term with you as the foster carer, this will have been discussed extensively with you during the care proceedings. Long-term foster care is the most common placement for children in the care system. Generally, 75–80% of children who are in the care system are in foster care. At the end of care proceedings, children who are to remain in long-term foster care are made subject to a care order under Section 31 of the 1989 Children Act. This means that parental responsibility is shared between the local authority and the birth parents but that the local authority has the lion's share and so can make decisions for the child without the consent of the birth parents. Most crucially the local authority decides where the child will be living and acts as the child's legal parent until they turn 18.

However, children do not see legal orders – they only see, and feel, the quality of the care, stability, consistency and love that they receive in the family they live in. Far too much can be made of the legal order that the child is on. In your foster home it really shouldn't matter whether the child is looked after under Section 20 of the 1989 Children Act or a full care order under Section 31.

So children who come into your care may stay in your care long term or may go on to one of the options outlined above. If they go on to a special guardianship order placement with a relative or on to adoption, then you will have a vital role to play in the transition of the child from your home to their new home where they will remain for the rest of their childhood.

Why do children come into the care system?

The most common reason that children enter the care system isn't sexual or physical abuse – it is neglect and the chaotic environment within the birth family. Often the parents are overwhelmed and struggle to prioritise the child. It is important to understand the experiences of the children you will look after. Chaotic households are often marked by inconsistency and a lack of stability, and both of these can have a profound impact on the child. It is likely that there are no real routines within the household the child may have come from, with mealtimes – even eating – not guaranteed. Discipline or care and control may be missing, with children getting different reactions to the same behaviour on different days. This is very confusing for them and can lead to behavioural issues. Children may not have had their emotional needs met, they were not comforted when they were sad, not fed when they were hungry and not tended to when they were hurt, and this lack of empathy and care from their parents can have very serious consequences. Stability, consistency and routine are critical to children as they move through their developmental stages.

It is important to understand that these early experiences do not need to define the rest of the child's life. As a foster carer the consistency, stability, love, predictability and commitment that you can offer to a child will go a very long way to helping them overcome traumatic and abusive experiences.

It is always important to consider and try to imagine the circumstances the child you are looking after may have come from when understanding or judging their behaviour when they arrive in your home. This behaviour may appear bizarre but would probably look perfectly normal if seen through the lens of the home they have come from. Common issues are those such as food hoarding when there is plenty of food in your house that they are allowed to have. It is more understandable when you realise that in the home that they have come from this was not the case and they perhaps did not know when they would next be fed. Simply knowing and being told that there is food and that they will always be fed and they can help themselves is often not enough to change this behaviour. It takes time for children to trust and understand that actually their needs will be met, that they will be cared for and that they will be fed, and a high degree of patience and tolerance is required by foster carers.

Foster carers also need the ability to offer a high degree of mentalisation. This is the ability to put yourself in the mind of the child, to understand what is going on inside their head and to understand why they react to the world in the way that they do. Gaining an understanding of this can help you become the child's second brain and aid them in navigating the sometimes overwhelming and unfathomable experiences that they have had.

What is always especially important to remember is that the information you might receive about the child you are to foster is not the whole story about who they are. By their very nature, social services files dwell on the negative and the traumatic things that have happened in children's lives. Our foster children constantly tell us that this isn't the whole story about who they are. The children you will foster may well have been traumatised or neglected and will need support and care to recover from this. However, they are also amazing, talented and wonderful, and full of potential to achieve success through their childhood and on into adult life.

Unaccompanied asylum-seeking children

A significant minority of the children that you may be asked to look after are unaccompanied asylum-seeking children.

Currently there are over 3000 unaccompanied asylum-seeking children in the UK residing in foster care. These are children who are in the UK completely unaccompanied by an adult, which means they have no parents, aunties, uncles or grandparents in the UK.

The children are seeking asylum. A dictionary definition of asylum is 'shelter or protection from danger'. These children have arrived in the UK fleeing countries impacted by war and other crises. They have left their families behind or have witnessed horrific violence and sometimes murder of their loved ones before making a terrifying journey to another country for shelter and protection. Often the children have stowed on boats and lorries to get to a new and strange country where they do not know what awaits, or the language spoken. These brave children need to be cared for within our fostering services.

> 'The young person we had in our care had endured quite an ordeal immediately before and during his journey into the UK. This was very challenging as it is impossible for many asylum-seeking young people to articulate this in the carer's mother tongue. We soon discovered that we needed to show the young person not only warmth and comfort, but we also had to prove he was in a safe place.'

Many of the young people we care for are boys aged between 11 and 17. When they arrive in the country, often little or nothing is known about them and a foster placement is found on this basis. Many foster carers say they are delighted that they have taken the decision to open their homes and lives to children and young people who are seeking asylum.

A main focus for these young people is to learn English. Some will have lived in several countries before entering the UK and have learned other languages and maybe some English either in their home countries or during their travels. Carers can use Google Translate, Language Line services and interpreters to help them communicate.

'When the young person came to us it was very difficult in the initial couple of days. The young person did not fully understand what was going on and we were trying to communicate with him the best we could. Unfortunately, this particular young person could not read in his own language so Google Translate was useless. What really struck me in the initial stages is how resourceful and resilient children can be, and we soon found it easy to communicate in hand signals and gestures. I think the general misconception with fostering asylum seekers is how difficult it is going to be to learn a new culture and language. Although this is difficult for the child, it also needs to be noted that it is just as much of a learning curve for the carer in most cases. Asylum seekers often have different religions, diets and views to those of the carer's.'

The children are adapting to a new culture and a new home when they enter foster care, and the carers need to be aware and sensitive to this. Like all children in foster care, their experiences and family life will undoubtedly have been different from their life now. Many of the young people have strong cultural values and religious beliefs, which need to be supported by their carers. Carers can spend time researching and meeting with people who can give them insight and information. Much of the detail comes from the children themselves as they are experts in their own lives and value base. Often this involves a change of diet within the family home, perhaps to incorporate halal foods and/or foods from the young person's country of origin. Young people may need to attend a mosque or other places of worship.

> *'The young person we have in our care is from Afghanistan and is a semi-practising Muslim. In day-to-day terms, it was a big challenge to adapt to a different routine. There are so many things to not only adapt to, but also to respect. Diet was a big change for us. The young person has a strict halal diet and, living rurally, we had to drive 25 miles to a city to buy varied halal food. We also had to ensure that any non-practising children in our care respected that, at times, the young person was not to be disturbed as he was praying. We also had to buy the young person a prayer mat. Culturally, there are many differences, and it is a balance trying to teach the young person our culture while respecting their culture.'*

Children seeking asylum in the UK require a solicitor who specialises in asylum applications. Foster carers will be required to support the children with the appointments so that they can complete the required documentation and applications accordingly. They will also be asked to attend a meeting at the Home Office with their carers. One of the major challenges for children seeking asylum is that they cannot apply for extended leave to remain in the country until they are over 17 years of age. This means that they may live with uncertainty for several years. How many of us would want to live with the knowledge and fear that we may be extradited from the country that we have considered home for much of our childhood?

> *'We found there to be many more appointments for an asylum-seeking young person than any other child in care. It is worth remembering that, in most cases, neither the young person nor social services can be 100% sure that they are up to date with all immunisations, and*

a full "MOT" is required. In effect, the young person is starting their medical history in the UK as if they were a baby, and in our case we found that a huge amount of injections were provided in a very short space of time. It is also worth noting that if a young person comes from a country where they suffer with illnesses that have pretty much died out in the UK, these will need to be screened and, if appropriate, treated.

In addition, the number of appointments that an asylum-seeking young person has with the social work team, solicitors and the Home Office is significant. The process starts with an age assessment from the local authority. This is followed by a screening interview at the Home Office in Croydon, where the young person is briefly interviewed, has photographs taken and declares their intent to seek asylum. The Home Office then sends out a letter, which includes a statement to be filled in by the young person. This really requires the help of a solicitor. In our case the closest solicitors are in the city, so that's another 50-mile round trip. The young person then has to wait for the Home Office to offer them a formal interview in Cardiff. One of the young people we have had six appointments cancelled as they could not find an interpreter, before eventually an interview took place. This is a very laborious task. There is a feeling that the interview with the Home Office can be very hard, and indeed our young person was very nervous. In between these meetings, dependent on the particular case, you may receive another letter from the Home Office to arrange for fingerprints to be taken at a post office that offers this service.'

For most, getting into education is a priority. Some young people find it challenging to undertake all subjects within the school curriculum as they are not able to speak the language in which the subject is being taught. Feedback from the young people and their carers has been that they are often highly competent in practical and vocational skills, which can be overlooked in the UK education system. It will be the carer's role to advocate on behalf of the young people they are caring for and ensure that their skills are nurtured and developed.

> *'Asylum-seeking young people in my care on the whole have found education very rewarding and they are often thankful to have this opportunity; I don't think we can ever underestimate how difficult it is for them. It can be hard for them to fit in, particularly if they are in a school where, in ethnicity terms, they are very much in the minority. We were very lucky as our local comprehensive has an amazing teacher who deals with children requiring learning support. Without him, the young people would be struggling a lot more than they are. We have had difficulty with some teachers expecting the young people to be doing exactly the same work as the rest of the class, but equally we have also had some fabulous teachers who have worked really hard to accommodate them and get the best out of them.'*

> *'The success you get from caring for unaccompanied asylum-seeking children by far outweighs the work. We have seen scared, lonely children grow in a short space of time to be confident, happy young men and women. One of the young people in our care came to us 11 months ago and could not speak a word of English and was extremely scared. Now he speaks extremely good English, has built up a very good circle of friends and is confident, with a great sense of humour.'*

There are many differences in looking after an asylum-seeking child compared with a child from the UK entering the care system. However, we must not forget the major similarity: they are all children – children who need care, support, empathy, understanding, patience, nurture, shelter and protection from danger…*a home.*

Conclusion

The children that you look after are likely to have had some challenging early childhood experiences. The effect of these can be quite profound, and you will see some of the difficulties that these have caused the children played out in your home. However, you have a unique opportunity to help these children recover from these experiences and to have a happy childhood and the chance of a successful transition to adult life.

Chapter 4

THROUGH THE EYES OF THE FOSTER CHILD

Andy Elvin and numerous foster children

Imagine you have been living at home with your parents. Home life may not always feel great or good or even safe, but it is all you've known and you don't really have anything to compare it with. Then adults called social workers become involved with your family's life, they visit your home, they talk to you and ask you questions about your family life, and they talk to your parents and sometimes to your teachers. One day you may find yourself having a conversation with one of these social workers who talks to you about the fact that you're going to live with someone else other than your parents for a while, that these people you're going to live with are called foster carers and that you may be going that very day to meet them and to live in their home.

How do you feel?

It is impossible to overstate how strange this situation must be to a child. The combination of hurt, fear, trepidation and anxiousness, and possibly also curiosity, can be overwhelming.

This child is going to arrive in your home one afternoon, probably with the social worker. The social worker may stay and talk to you, and your own supervising social worker agency may also be present to support you, but at some point after an hour or so they're going to leave you alone with your foster child.

Foster children say that one of the most frustrating things when they arrive in a foster home is that foster parents don't even know basic things about what they like, what they don't like or what their interests are. It can also be quite frustrating that the foster carers seem to be walking on eggshells around them for fear of how they might behave or what they might do. Honesty really is the best policy. Ask your foster child questions about what they like and what they don't like in terms of food or TV and what they might like to do. Make sure that the child has permission to say the things they like and don't like, and reassure them that they won't offend you, that you'll be getting to know each other and it's okay to say the ways they prefer things to be. Fostering is about relationships, and the best relationships are built on honesty and clear and open communication, so that's the best way to start every placement.

Humans are social beings – therefore the feeling of belonging is essential to all children and young people, not least to those in our care. Having somewhere to call home and feeling accepted, safe and secure is founded on belonging. Feeling a part of something helps young people recover from and deal with past hurt and trauma and develop positive and trusting relationships. Belonging builds self-confidence and self-belief. Here's what foster children say:

'Sometimes the rule that you can't do a specific thing isolates you, like when I was younger I wasn't allowed to sleep out.'

'I don't want to be part of a family; I have my own family.'

Young people are the experts on their own experience; they have a right to be heard, like anyone else. Being heard helps young people to explore and make sense of their feelings and experiences, feel a sense of control over their own lives and develop lifelong communication skills.

By listening, we can better understand their aspirations and ambitions and make decisions that best fit with young people's own views and preferences.

Over to our children again:

> 'It mattered to me that I didn't have any food or clothes before I came here and I was able to tell my carer and she bought me some. She bought me a new uniform and in my mind I fell in love with it because it was so smart and I'd never had one before.'

> 'I am allowed to express my opinion, which is something I couldn't do when I lived at home.'

> 'Sometimes what I am thinking is not realistic. My carer listens to my opinion and will support me if she can.'

> 'Adults make the decisions...young people do not always have much say.'

> 'I feel I should be allowed to make more decisions so I can learn from my mistakes and mess up if that's what may happen.'

All children deserve a loving and happy home. Care can be transformational, giving a young person a safe and secure place to recover from past trauma, be a child, grow and develop, and discover who they are. Care offers young people new experiences and opportunities that encourage their aspirations and ambitions and enable them to succeed. Most of all, care shows young people that adults believe in them and will speak up for them. All of this leads to better long-term outcomes for young people.

In a recent TACT survey 82% of young people felt that being in care was the right thing for them, compared with 62% who thought that coming into care was the right thing at the time they came into care. This illustrates the changing perceptions of children and young people. Often children's only experience of family life is with their birth family and so foster care can be a significant contrast. Often, though children are still loyal to and love their parents they appreciate being in foster care.

For young people it is important that they meet their carers before they move in with them, as this helps with the transition:

> 'We met twice and so it was easier to move in and not a big shock, as we had time to talk and get to know one another.'

> 'I had some time to think and make decisions about moving in with her.'

What makes a good carer?

Foster care can transform outcomes for vulnerable children. According to children and young people a good foster carer is:

> '...patient, energetic, respectful, committed, supportive, empathic, a good listener, caring and nurturing, a good communicator and good humoured. But most of all a good carer wants the best for the children they look after.'

We often say to potential carers that it is about having room in your house but, more importantly, room in your heart.

Education

School is a big part of children's lives, and it is vital that foster carers are engaged with their child's education. Here's what children say:

> 'I was always open about being in care but I always felt different from the other children. It was the little things, and because I was open about my situation, the teachers referred to me being in care on occasion. I think the teachers could be more sensitive.'

'I think some do [understand the needs of looked-after children] and some don't. There are ones that don't need to learn, but I think in the teacher training days they should have a day where they listen to the experiences of kids in care. I would do it, tell them about me.'

'Yes I do [feel that teachers understand the needs of looked-after children]. If I get upset, they will help me and ask me what's wrong.'

'Teachers need to be more patient.'

'Counsellors tried to work with us to get us to stop messing about. They really made me think about things like getting inside my head. I'd leave their room with a headache from thinking too much about stuff. But it helps me as I think about stuff all the time, why things happen to me.'

'There was a counsellor who I used to go to talk to, but then she left and no one replaced her. I knew her well and found it easy to talk to her.'

'Pupil learning support is helpful, understands what I need, and helped sort out a college day every week.'

Many children in care say they are made to feel different in school. Things like being pulled out frequently for looked-after children or personal education plan meetings, missing class for services, perceived stigmatisation by teachers, language barriers, cultural differences, bullying, falling behind in coursework and unwanted special attention from teachers all make them feel different. This is what they say:

'In primary it was really hard. Having meetings all the time makes you different. I used to feel rubbish some days and found school really hard.'

'Yes [I feel my educational experience is different], but in a good way. I think being in care gives you more opportunities than other children have.'

'My teachers know that I am in care and understand me, but I am treated the same as everyone else.'

'I think there is a lot of favouritism and I am not treated equally. Some teachers make judgements. They should have more empathy.'

'Yes [I fell behind], because of the amount of school I missed before I came into care. It took a few years for me to catch up, but I did it with the support of my school and carers.'

'I have had a lot of appointments like play therapy, physiotherapy, orthodontist and meetings and had to be off school.'

'You have to be loud and clear and then you are heard. It is easier when you are older and get help to make yourself heard.'

'I sometimes go to my personal education plan meetings, but sometimes I am not asked. I would go if I was asked to.'

'I haven't been to my personal education plan meeting this year. I would go if I was invited.'

'I don't think my teachers listened to me, but I felt supported by everyone else.'

Having foster carers who are engaged with their foster child's education makes a big difference. Here are a few children telling us how much of a difference:

'I think [my carer] does everything she possibly can for me. I just wish I'd moved to hers sooner, perhaps I would have achieved more than I did.'

'We do my homework together. My carers also make sure that I get one-to-one tuition in maths.'

'They are amazing. [My carer] helps me with everything; anything that comes up I just need to ask her. She asks

me every day how school is and knows what's going on. They go to every parents' night, stuff at the school, they get involved. She has talked through [education] plans with me and helped me. They want the best for me.'

Listening to and involving children and young people

It is also important to both listen to and involve children and young people. Good agencies and local authorities involve young people in staff recruitment, panels and training, and train and support them to undertake this role.

TACT regularly surveys its children and young people. The delivery of the latest survey in 2015 was overseen by the TACT Children's Champions group, a group of young people who meet regularly to discuss and review issues that are important to them. This revealed a lot about the young people. Here are some of the headline statistics:

- 94% of young people feel able to express their opinions about things that matter to them.

- 87% of young people rated their foster carer as good or very good.

- 96% of young people said that their carer makes them feel good about themselves.

- 89% of young people spend leisure time with their foster carers and enjoy being with them.

- 95% of young people feel part of their carer's family because they feel included.

'My carers are the only family who have ever treated me as as they would their own.'

'I feel that being in foster care is helping me achieve what I want to be in later life and giving me lots of options.'

Before choosing which agency or local authority to foster for, ask how they include and listen to the children and young people in their care.

CASE STUDY

Being in care for me was and still is a mix of negatives and positives thrown together. Other young people always ask what it is like, and the best way I can describe it is that for whatever reason you cannot go home and have to live with people who are essentially strangers to you. They're usually quite disappointed to hear that it's nothing like *Tracy Beaker*.

I think one thing potential foster carers and foster carers should keep in mind is giving the young person space and time. You may mean well by checking on them every half an hour, but being in a new household with people they have never met before will take some time for them to get used to, and repeatedly checking on them will most likely push them away. This is something I wish some of my previous carers had kept in mind.

I use a wheelchair, and one of my previous carers really treated me differently because of this. I don't think they meant any harm but I really could have done without it. I was 15 and wasn't even allowed to go to the corner shop to get some chocolate. I mean, as if I was going to run away!

Foster carers should see the young person for themselves, not their disability or health condition, get to know them as a person, and not just assume they have a low level of independence and intelligence because their legs don't work. I mean, David Weir didn't even have legs, and look at what he managed to do.

This one relates back to getting to know the young person. One of my carers really got to know me and remembered things I said. For example, I must have mentioned I get really bad dandruff, and when she went shopping later that week she picked me up some anti-dandruff shampoo. It's the little things.

I would suggest that, if you have children of your own, whatever you do don't leave out the fostered young person. For example, if every year at Easter your children get an Easter egg, get them one too. If around Christmas all your children get advent calendars, get them one too. It's not the egg or advent calendar they are after, it's the fact you included them in the household unit.

The last thing I would say is I have a very strong opinion about carers learning about different religions and backgrounds. As a foster carer you will be taking care of children and young people of different ethnicities, backgrounds, religions and possibly even nationalities, so I think it is essential that you have a basic knowledge, such as what halal meat is or what kosher meat is. Obviously, I'm not saying that foster carers should know everything because they will learn as they meet more young people, but they should at least have a basic knowledge and be eager to learn more.

CASE STUDY

Coming into care can be an extremely emotional time for any young person but it can also be an enjoyable experience; moving placements is also very hard.

Although it can be very tough for any young person in care, the foster carers and social workers are there with you every step of the way. Personally I have had fun so far – being in care isn't as tough as people make out.

I have been included in everything my foster carers have done. They have made foster care very pleasant and have included me in various activities, which I have found myself enjoying immensely. My foster carers have made my life a whole lot easier in terms of me being able to act my age rather than like someone ten times older than me. Also they have helped me learn to relax and not put myself under pressure just because I'm not used to the situation.

The children's co-ordinator has been very supportive with every child in care, including me! I have had an extremely hard time being in care in the past, but when I was first introduced to the agency that my carers foster for I was in awe of how successful they are and how big they are – they have branches all over the country! My foster carers are very inspiring; they have taught me to be myself and that you can achieve anything if you try.

One of the questions I have been asked many times at school is, 'Is being in care like *Tracy Beaker*?' The answer is 'No!' That is a TV show and we are real, not on a TV show, and our life isn't that chaotic.

So my advice to people coming into care is to be yourself – don't worry what people say about you just because you are in care, and when people tell you to reach for the sky just think, why are you telling me this when I know there are footprints on the moon?

Conclusion

The children that you will care for are amazing. They are talented, funny and wise and will constantly surprise you in good and sometimes interesting ways. Remember that they are not just the sum of the difficult experiences they have had and that the bleak picture that the information you receive about them may paint is not the whole story.

Your foster children will have aspirations, hopes and dreams. It is your job to understand these and to help your children achieve them.

Chapter 5

YOUR FIRST PLACEMENT
—— Martin Barrow ——

It can take between four and six months to be approved as a foster carer. But the reality is that for many fostering families the journey to foster care takes much longer, sometimes several years.

It begins as a random conversation, inspired by a film, or a book, or a chance meeting with a foster carer. It is a thought, an aspiration that is tucked away for another day, for when the time is right. You hear advertisements on the radio and read articles in the local newspaper about foster carers, and look into it in more detail, yet still the timing is not right. Your children are too young, the family home is not suitable, work (and life in general) is too complicated. But as weeks become months, those radio commercials continue to play, and the obstacles to becoming foster carers are no longer intractable.

You make the first move, attending an open evening, and meet families who have the same aspirations as you, and the same anxieties. You realise that they have gone through a similar process and, like you, are slightly surprised to find themselves signing up for the approval process. You attend the courses, submit to the interviews, and present yourselves to a fostering panel. When you leave the building, you leave as foster carers.

It is a huge moment: you are excited, proud even. And not a little frightened, as the responsibility of what you have signed up to begins to sink in. In the immediate aftermath, I remember having doubts about whether we would be up to the challenge, or whether what we were proposing was actually fair on other members of the family, not least on our own children.

We began to see our home through different eyes, spotting previously unnoticed dangers, even though we had already invested considerable time and money in addressing safety concerns.

Once we were approved we wanted our first placement to begin as quickly as possible, to prove to ourselves that we were capable of rising to the challenge. We also wanted to show the fostering team that they were right to have faith in us as a fostering family.

How long you have to wait for the first placement depends on a number of circumstances, including the local need for foster carers, and the parameters you have set for the children you are ready to look after. You will have the opportunity to agree a range of ages, or whether you will have boys or girls (or both). Physical and mental disabilities should be a consideration, particularly for your first experience of foster care. Distances you are prepared to travel, for school or parental contact, are important. Do you have pets? The more versatile you are, the shorter you are likely to have to wait for the first placement. Nonetheless, some new foster carers wait several weeks for their placement, while others are kept busy from the moment they are approved.

The assessment process for foster carers can feel intrusive and over-complicated at times. But it does give the fostering team the chance to get to know your strengths, and the type of children who will be a good match for you and your family. Their understanding of your capabilities, and your stated preferences, should limit the scope for surprises when the first placement arrives.

Family history

Before accepting your first placement as foster carer you will have access to the child's family history, which will also explain the reason why they were taken into care. The level of information available will depend on the length of time a child has been known to social workers. A children's department may have been providing support to a family for an extended period before a decision is taken to place the children in care. Or a child may previously have been in care but returned to the family home, only for a further intervention to be considered necessary. It is also possible that a child has been living with another foster family but there are reasons why this placement cannot continue.

Under these circumstances, foster carers will be provided with a significant amount of information about the children who may come to live with them. It is important for you to read these notes very carefully. Be warned that the notes can contain information about the children that you may find distressing, so it is advisable not to read them alone. The notes are written in a factual way, and collated from information provided by a wide range of people, from social workers and health visitors to police and teachers.

The notes will inform you about the child's relationship with the birth family, particularly parents and siblings; about living conditions; about physical and emotional health; about educational attainment; and about the child's life outside the family home, including significant friendships and leisure interests.

You will also learn about the level of deprivation the child has endured, and about any injuries. You will read about emotional abuse as well as physical. It is possible that this abuse has taken place over an extended period, before it came to the notice of the authorities.

The standard of these notes does vary according to the information that is available but also depending on the care that has been taken to document a child's history. Sometimes there will be gaps, and sometimes the information does not add up. Do not be afraid to ask questions, or to request additional information that has not been included in the notes. Experienced foster carers learn to assume that a child's history will be even more complicated than the notes suggest, and that the level of difficulty will be more severe than the information implies.

When possible, try to speak to people who have had contact with the child, such as the social worker or previous foster carer, rather than relying on the notes alone. Encourage them to tell you positive things about the child, and not just the issues of concern. Sometimes a child makes significant progress during the first few weeks in care, simply by virtue of being removed from conflict, and eating and sleeping well. So, notes may already be slightly out of date, and the child's previous carer will hold invaluable information about what has already made a profound difference.

You may be asked to read notes about a number of children from different placements, which can expose you to harrowing details of cases that you will subsequently hear nothing more about. This is because you may be put forward as the proposed carer in a case that is then resolved in a different way. Sometimes information comes to light during a care application that affects the outcome. The outcome itself may not be known until just hours before the child is due to arrive at your home. This can be upsetting, as well as frustrating, especially if you have spent time getting ready for the arrival, or have prepared your own children to welcome a particular child. But the decision is taken in the child's best interests.

Ideally, you will have time to consider the notes, raise questions about the case, make arrangements with family and home and be ready to welcome the new arrival. What's more, the child will have been told about you and your family, and may have been shown photographs of you.

It won't always be like this, and foster carers must quickly learn to be adaptable, above all else. We have learned to take nothing for granted until the doorbell rings and children are delivered safely into our care.

A positive outcome is particularly important for new foster carers. A difficult placement at the beginning of your lives as carers can have a detrimental impact on you and your family, as well as on the child who has been placed in your care. It is important that you feel supported, and that you are equipped to accept the challenge. Just as you have the right to ask for more information, you also should feel empowered to say no if you feel that the first placement you are being offered is not right for you and your family. Of course, this remains true for all foster carers, but new foster carers, sometimes through a lack of experience or because of their eagerness to get started, may go along with an arrangement that is not right. Be firm and raise any concerns that you have. Make sure that the right support is actually in place, rather than brushed off as something to be discussed at a later stage. This is your moment to influence the terms of the placement.

By looking after yourselves, you will be doing your best for the child. This is important to remember for as long as you are foster carers. Even as you rush around to get everything ready in the final hours before your first placement begins, make time for you and your family. Think about going out for a meal together, or to the cinema. Maybe take a long walk as a family, or order a takeaway and play games. Fostering does not mean that you won't ever be able to do this again, of course, but inevitably there will be fewer opportunities. If you have your own children it is also a good moment to tell them how proud you are of them. Sometimes we forget that we foster as a family, and that our sons and daughters make sacrifices to find room in their lives for other people's children.

You should also remind yourself that your home, for all its imperfections and peculiarities, is safe. It is also warm and dry, and there is food on the table. But above all, it is a safe haven away from the dangers and strife that most children who come into care have faced every day. Yes, the colour of the bedroom walls matters, and maybe the lampshade is a bit faded. But what foster children are most likely to remember, years later, will be the fresh, clean sheets and pillow, or the warm greeting when they come home from school, or the bedtime story at the end of the day.

But final preparations are undoubtedly important. If you are expecting a young child, think of the toys and games they will enjoy. Consider which rooms in the house the child can play in, and move treasured items out of reach of little hands. Younger children tend to follow you around, particularly in the early days, so give thought to how you might manage this, particularly in the kitchen. Older boys and girls will want space of their own and are likely to spend more time in their bedrooms. How practical is this? Does the room have a TV, and does the wi-fi work in there? Where will the child do homework? They will need far more support than you might have been used to with your own children, so make a room where you can be available, even when you are busy with the household chores. If you are awaiting the arrival of a baby, make sure that you have enough nappies of different sizes, in case the information you have is already out of date.

The arrival

Each time a foster child arrives it is a unique and special experience. It is a critical moment, which can set the tone for the duration of the placement. As new foster carers, you will be both excited and apprehensive. But your mixed emotions will be nothing compared with the child's.

If the child has just been placed in care, it is possible that they are coming to your home against their will, so they may be angry and hostile, as well as scared. The child may be unable to understand the reasons why they have been separated from their birth family. No matter how much children have been neglected or abused, physically or emotionally, they will want to go back to mum and dad. If the police or health services were involved, they will be anxious about their parents' safety and well-being. They may also blame themselves for what has happened. They will have, at best, a hazy idea of where they actually are in relation to their home. They are probably only just beginning to process the implications of what this means in terms of their school, their friends and their extended family. They are unlikely to know whether they are staying with you for days, weeks or even months.

You must not judge the child based on their arrival or appearance. You are strangers; what's more, in their eyes you probably represent the same authority that broke up their family. Under these circumstances of a sudden and extreme change, you cannot expect too much from a newly arrived child. There will be no instant connection.

Managing this tension requires a deft touch, and no small amount of compassion. Our preference is for children to arrive during the day, partly because they are likely to be less tired than at the end of the day but also because our house, in a semi-rural location, can seem intimidating at night time.

How we welcome children depends on the nature of the placement. As the main carer, my wife will always be present. Generally, I will also be there. Sometimes we encourage our daughters to join us, but we also are mindful that a small crowd can be intimidating. Having another child present can help to break the ice, particularly if the foster child is very young.

Food and mealtimes

Food and mealtimes are frequently major issues in foster care. Children who have not been fed regularly or consistently bring with them a survival mentality towards food. They are inclined to hoard food, or to overeat when it is available, and fret over the next meal even when they have a full stomach. Some children gorge themselves and eat until they are sick.

They will not be used to seeing food stored in cupboards or in the refrigerator, and might steal food to hide in their bedroom. They feel less anxious if they store food for later. It is not unusual for children in care to ask, just before they go to sleep, what they will be having for breakfast the following morning. When breakfast is finished, they will ask what lunch will be, and so on. 'Food', when it was available at home, often meant chips, so they may have a craving for junk food that is difficult to satisfy. By the same measure, they may reject foods that are alien to them, including vegetables and fruit.

Food can become the subject of a complex struggle for control. It can be further complicated if children have no eating skills or table manners. It is not unusual to care for children with no, or limited, experience of sitting at a table and using a knife and fork. This can be highly disruptive of your own mealtimes. However, it is important for children to observe how you eat food and conduct yourself at the table. They will learn from your example. So, try to share mealtimes, even if you don't do it every day.

This anxiety over food is likely to be a part of their lives well into adulthood, and without the right support it can develop into eating disorders that will require medical treatment. As a foster carer, you are in a position to help them begin the journey towards understanding, and trusting, food. But it will require patience and perseverance. Progress will be uneven, influenced by anxiety arising from the crises that inevitably come with being in foster care.

Trust your instinct, but do not hesitate to seek advice from a medical professional if you are concerned.

In the early days, be prepared to compromise between the food they *will* eat and the food they *should* eat. Show how you enjoy foods that they might not be familiar with, and encourage them to begin with tiny helpings. Be explicit about the foods that you will not serve in the house, and explain why. Never use food as a punishment.

Involve the children in cooking and baking. It is fun and an essential life skill. It also helps to break down any concerns they have about food. Many of the children we have cared for have no understanding of where their food comes from. Preparation of vegetables and fruit for cooking provides an opportunity to talk about food, and gives children a real sense of achievement when something they have cooked or baked is served at mealtimes. It also helps to involve the children in shopping for food, when you can talk about why you make certain choices and what you plan to make with the ingredients you buy. This is the sort of early instruction that many of their own parents missed out on when they were younger.

School

We often say that the success of a foster placement is secured at the school gate. It is here that a foster carer can make connections with the parents of your foster child's classmates that can be converted into invitations for tea, or birthday parties and sleepovers. These are essential building blocks for a child or young person's social life.

But it can be tough. If a child continues at the same school, there may be some hostility towards you from mums and dads who know the birth family. Some will mistrust you, because they do not differentiate between foster carers and social workers, and mistrust you as an extension of the local authority. Others will know your foster child's family by reputation, and will give you a wide berth. These are barriers that must be overcome, but it is not easy. Sometimes it requires help from the teaching staff, particularly if unfounded rumours have been spread about why the children have been taken into care.

Often the best way to break down barriers is through the children themselves. A child who is suffering neglect or abuse at home is more likely to be bullied and also to be a bully. They struggle academically and have few friends. Removal from a tough environment at home should be the catalyst for change. In my experience, a child or young person in foster care can make quick and significant progress simply by arriving at school looking smart and clean, with well-kempt hair, a new school bag and energised by a proper breakfast.

Classmates are quick to spot the difference and keen to be seen with a kid who is suddenly cooler, smarter and happier. Parents feel the vibe and become curious about the new set-up, which sparks those important conversations at the school gate. Once they realise that it is safe to engage, marvellous things can happen.

Some schools are better than others at responding to having a child in care. It may come down simply to previous experience and having a protocol in place which is understood by all teaching staff. Other schools can be defensive, particularly if there is a suggestion that there were failings in their own safeguarding procedures. Either way, it is important for a foster carer to engage with the school at the earliest opportunity. The headteacher needs to be informed of the change of guardianship, and staff must be made aware of the difficult period their pupil is living through.

More importantly, they all need to know that you, as a foster carer, will spare no effort to make sure that your foster child gets all the support they need to achieve, and even exceed, expected levels of attainment. Teachers are usually galvanised by the fresh start and willing to go the extra yard if they know that their efforts are reciprocated at home.

Health

Children in care are more likely to have physical and mental health problems as a consequence of their experiences. They may have suffered severe neglect and lived in substandard accommodation which has caused or aggravated underlying health conditions. Poor diet and personal hygiene are contributory factors. They also suffer because of their birth family's inability to manage a child's health condition, or through poor access to medical care.

A child's health needs should be given the utmost priority when a placement begins. It is important to remember that fostering, unlike an adoption or a residence order, does not transfer parental responsibility to a foster carer. So, the parents must be involved in decisions around medical treatment.

However, the foster carer can and should take a lead in seeking medical attention for the children in their care. This should be done in partnership with social workers and with the birth parents. In practice, this means taking children for routine appointments to the doctor, dentist or optician. When children need to see a specialist, it is incumbent on the foster carer to ensure that appointments are secured and kept. The key is to ensure that you inform the children's social worker, who is responsible for discussions with the parents.

It is often the case that a routine appointment may be the first time a child has been seen by a GP for several months, or longer. So, this is an important opportunity for a thorough health check, and to agree a course of action if care or treatment is needed. The same applies to visits to the dentist.

Some of the health issues you have to deal with will be complex and serious. Although you may have some experience of managing paediatric conditions, you may not have a medical background, so it is vital to seek advice from healthcare professionals. Keep a record of these contacts, and of the advice they give you, in case of any subsequent challenge, particularly by the child's birth family.

You can make a profound difference simply by applying the same standards that you do for yourself and your children. You are able to advocate on their behalf, in a way that the birth family could not. You are also likely to find strong support from healthcare professionals for the work that you are doing as a foster carer. They, like you, want only the best for your child.

Bathroom routines, hygiene and belongings

Give thought to bathroom routines, particularly to the need for privacy. Obviously, life is easier if you have more than one bathroom, but that won't always be the case. It is extremely important for children to feel safe, and private, when they are washing and dressing and going to the toilet. You and other members of the family will have to wear appropriate clothing at all times to avoid embarrassment. In foster care, bath time is particularly important for younger children in helping them to trust an adult, and it is good to establish a routine as early as possible in the placement. This is often the moment when children talk openly about their concerns and past experiences, so be prepared for difficult, emotional conversations in the bathroom.

Children often come into care with a very limited understanding of the importance of personal hygiene. Even older children may need help with some of the most basic aspects of personal care. They may not be used to washing or brushing their teeth. They may not use the toilet properly. Bathroom fittings that are not securely fixed are likely to be pulled apart. Children will go through extraordinary quantities of toilet paper. And remember to make sure that the bathroom door can be unlocked from the outside.

Be ready to respond to bedwetting. Even children with no previous history of bedwetting can lapse as a consequence of the upset caused by being removed from their family. Some children wet themselves during the night simply because they have never been told not to. But most learn very quickly with the right support and encouragement, which, in turn, is a real confidence booster when it comes to addressing other issues. In the meantime, cover mattresses with protective undersheets and have a good supply of spare sheets, duvets and blankets.

Children and young people generally arrive with very little. Their belongings often fit in a small holdall, or a couple of carrier bags. What they do bring is very precious to them and should be treated with respect, even though items of clothing or shoes may be threadbare and worn. Their clothes remind them of home – they smell of home, which brings comfort. Belongings frequently get lost in transit, which can cause distress to the children as well as leaving them without important items, so it is best to assume that you will have to provide everything they need (flannels, toothbrush, pyjamas, underwear, socks, slippers and so on). Do all that you can to try to recover items that have been left behind in cars and waiting rooms, and let the children see that you are already fighting on their behalf.

Although we assume that a child will arrive with precious little, we don't stock up on everything we need in advance. Instead, we like to go shopping with children to give them the opportunity to choose things like clothes and toys. Often it is the first time that somebody has actually asked them what *they* want or given them a choice. They have a voice and they are being heard. Thus, an everyday experience like shopping can become the beginning of a journey towards empowerment.

Keeping a written record

There is nothing in the assessment process that quite prepares you for the amount of paperwork that comes with being a foster carer.

You are required to keep a diary to record each day's events. The sorts of things you might write about include improvements and achievements, happy moments, first words, or a commendation at school. You should also record changes in behaviour or mood, setbacks and what was happening in the build-up to a crisis, and how you responded.

It can be a challenge to keep the diary up to date, but it is an essential part of foster care. Your diary serves as a history for the child or young person. It is also used to inform care planning. Your records may provide evidence for what triggers particular behaviour, how children respond to contact or whether a particular way of working with the child is producing the desired outcome. They also give an opportunity to reflect on a child's progress.

Your records may also be used in court proceedings. The information gleaned from your diary may influence the decisions that are taken regarding permanency for the child.

Some days there will not be much to add, but other days' entries will require time and thought, particularly when you are recording events or conversations that caused distress. It can be upsetting to relive these moments. Because your days will be so full, diary writing tends to get left until the late evening, when the children are asleep. That means you end up writing them just before your own bedtime, and find that your own sleep is disturbed as you keep going over what you have just written. Over the period of an extended placement this is not sustainable, so try to make time for diary notes earlier in the day, particularly when you know there are difficult moments to record, and do something nice before bedtime.

Even if you keep your diary up to date, you must still inform social workers immediately of any concerns you have over a particular incident, rather than wait for them to read your diary.

Footnote

We found our first placement enormously challenging. It involved a young teenager who had suffered neglect in a family with a history of alcoholism. She was angry and confused. Although she did not feel safe living at home, she had a strong bond with her family and found it difficult to be apart from them. Despite her young age, she was already a heavy smoker. She was doing poorly at school, had little interest in school work and habitually played truant.

For us as new foster carers, this was always going to be a tough placement, but we were determined to show her that this could be her home, and that our family would make room for her as one of our own. She ran away on several occasions, only to be returned by the police, and struggled to settle. Yet we could see small, positive changes that suggested to us that we were making a difference.

With the benefit of experience we can now recognise the mistakes that we made during that first placement, which could not be compensated for by our undoubted determination to be loving and compassionate foster carers.

Sadly, the placement came to an unexpected and sudden end when my wife Lorna was diagnosed with cancer, requiring urgent treatment. For our foster child, it felt like a betrayal that we should ask her to leave. She was too young, and too vulnerable, to understand the seriousness of my wife's condition.

Lorna made a full recovery, and a year later we were fostering again, this time for three siblings. During her treatment we promised ourselves that we would return to fostering. We both felt that we had let down our first foster child, and the memory of her difficult departure still troubles us.

CASE STUDY

Our first fostering experience

We received our first proper placement of Darren and John in December 2012. We had three children of our own: Marcus aged ten, Daniel aged six, and Carl aged two. John was 17 months old and Darren had just turned four years old the previous month. John had only been crawling for four weeks and as yet couldn't walk. We were told that the boys were so neglected that Darren used to use a broom handle to knock food down from a cupboard to eat when they were hungry, and the nursery that Darren had attended had made referrals to the council regarding his welfare. The nursery said that he was always in unclean clothes and told them every day that he had not had any breakfast. It was believed that they were often left alone in the house while their mum was out overnight. Darren told me that he and John would often wake up alone and that he would climb into the cot with John to play with him until his mum returned.

Their mother had a drug and alcohol addiction. She was also involved in a domestic abuse relationship and had left the boys home alone while she visited the local A&E department after a physical fight with her boyfriend which had left her face in need of medical treatment and an x-ray. The police visited her address several times but Darren had been told to hide when someone came to the door. The police finally saw Darren through a window eating a yoghurt. They asked him to let them into the property. Darren was able to open the door for them to gain access and they found John in his pushchair facing the wall. The police took the children to the police station and bought them fish and chips from the chip shop nearby. This is a memory that Darren carried with him for the next few years he spent with us.

The boys were placed into emergency foster care with a local carer. She already had two young children in placement, and when Darren and John arrived she had four children all under the age of four. Darren quickly found that to get as much attention as the younger children he had to behave just like them and sometimes poo in his pants in the morning as the other babies did in their nappies. He would be cleaned up with baby wipes and he enjoyed this attention from the carer. When we received the phone call from our social worker about Darren and John, Steven and I decided to take the boys into our home. We drove up to meet the boys and we were to pick them up a few days later and bring them home with us. When we first met Darren he was very over-friendly and wanted us to play with him straightaway. He especially liked doing jigsaws. There were boxes and boxes of toys the foster carer had collected over the years, all very tidily put into stacking boxes. We were shocked at so many boxes of toys for small children. Darren wanted to sit on our knees and was not shy. A little later the male foster carer brought John down from his nap and he called John a 'little treasure'. John was not shy and he crawled over to us and wanted to be picked up by us holding his hands up. We were shocked to hear the stories of neglect that these two little boys had suffered.

Darren and John were having contact with their mum three days per week, transported there by the contact worker who supervised contact. A few days later they were home with us, and the next morning Darren had soiled his pants again. I devised a reward chart that soon put an end to this behaviour. The boys soon made friends with our son Carl, who was two at the time, and they became great friends over the next two years. Steven and I used to call them the Three Musketeers as they were so close.

We took them on holiday to Turkey and for the first time the boys went on an aeroplane; they were very good and slept for most of the flight. On holiday it was enjoyable but with stressful points. John messed himself twice in the evening after dinner, which was tough to clean up in an unfamiliar place.

During the two years that they stayed with us John learned to walk and Darren started nursery in our village, then went into Reception and Year 1. Darren was very bright and did not struggle with his school work. He was, however, very needy and desperate to please everyone, but he could be destructive and loud too. John started nursery a little while later and his attention-seeking behaviour was not easy for the nursery staff to cope with. John made a big hole in the wall of the nursery from repeatedly bashing a wooden trolley against it until the plaster came off. He moved to the village nursery when he was three years old and they managed his behaviour much better there, but he still tried to escape through doors regularly, and frequently held his hands up to be picked up.

The care plan was for the boys to be moved on to adoption after the birth mother was ruled out of their lives due to her lack of commitment and ongoing problems. No suitable family members were able to come forward to take the boys. The boy's mum had another baby, this time a little girl, and she was to be placed with the boys for adoption with a couple who had had fertility problems and had been through four failed IVF attempts. Adoption was their only hope to have children. The couple both worked full time but were willing to change their work commitments to have children.

There was a very carefully devised plan to enable this to happen, which had been tested time and time again with other cases. This included meetings with child and adolescent mental health services, where Darren and John would talk about meeting a new mum and dad who would be special to them and would always look after them properly. There were counselling sessions for Darren with discussions about his past life with his mum, how things were with us and how they might be with his new mum and dad. John was too young for this level of discussion, so he had a separate play session. I found one of these sessions very emotional as we talked about the boys leaving our home and how we would miss them. It was brought home to me that they would soon be leaving us and I didn't want Darren to see me cry, but the counsellor said that Darren should see my emotions. He tried to comfort me by saying that I could visit him. I felt that Carl needed this kind of help also, and I was worried about how he would deal with the loss of his two foster brothers. A two-week rota was devised whereby the boys would spend a careful amount of time with their new parents, which would increase every day, starting at our house and transitioning to time at their new home before the big day.

Every day some of the boys' things would be transported over to their new home. It was sad to see the bikes go as they had played on them together so much in the back garden with Carl. I attended a big meeting at the social services offices where all the professionals and the new parents were invited. I was upset to discover a recommendation to change John's first name to a name chosen by the adoptive parents. It was felt that there was a risk of their birth mother tracking them down. So many people knew him as John. His photo album and his memory box was full of things which said 'John'. This was extremely difficult for me to process and I took a break from the meeting to compose myself. John called me 'Mum' during his time with us and I tried to discourage this, but he was my little John and I felt like his mum. I made my feelings clear, as I didn't agree that there was a risk. Their birth mother had no home and had become lost in drugs. She no longer had access to the boys and wasn't even trying to see them. My social worker was there for me professionally and emotionally, for which I was grateful. I was told that I couldn't visit the boys at their new home because they would think that I was going to take them away from there, so we had to meet on neutral ground if we were to keep in contact.

For the next few weeks the boys said goodbye to their friends at school and Darren found this emotional. We started the meetings with the new parents and things went well. I thought they were a nice couple and pretty 'normal'. I was glad for them and for the boys to finally have what they deserved, a family. The big day arrived; Darren and John said goodbye to Marcus, Daniel and Carl with hugs and kisses. My friend Kim came with me to take them; she wanted to be there for me as she knew it would be difficult for me. Darren was excited and he wanted to show me his bedroom and John's bedroom straightaway. I was there with the boys' social worker and we chatted and had a coffee, and then I felt that it was time for me to leave. I hugged and kissed the boys and then left, hoping that I would see them soon. I came out of there feeling devastated, but pleased for their new ready-made family. I only saw the boys once after that at a play barn, but I kept in contact through messages and pictures for a short time. Carl developed a stammer in his speech after they left, and the consultant said it was because he was so used to talking with his foster brothers on that level and now he had to talk on an adult level; it took some months before he was able to talk properly.

Conclusion

You will never forget your first placement. You will learn so much, and what you learn will carry through every subsequent placement that you have. Never be afraid to ask for help and support, from your social worker and from fellow foster carers. Fostering is a relationship, a two-way process, and you will learn as much from your foster children as they will learn and take from you. This starts with your first placement, so be open to this learning and be open to the fact that you may have to adapt and change your approach because your child has taught you that there are many ways to be a good and effective parent.

Chapter **6**

TRAINING AND BEHAVIOUR MANAGEMENT
—— Martin Clarke ——

Why do I need to do further learning?

When you go to a garage you expect the mechanics to be aware of how the new technology works in your car, don't you? When you go to the doctor or dentist you expect them to be up to date on new drugs, techniques and practices, don't you? When you see a police officer you anticipate them knowing the laws, including all the recent ones, don't you? Similarly, when you go to see any professional (solicitor, estate agent, accountant), you expect that they know their subject…so why should foster carers be any different?

As a foster carer you are a professional. You are a childcare professional and should expect to be treated as such by other professionals you come into contact with, such as social workers, teachers and health workers. However, to be a professional brings with it the expectation that you will keep yourself updated on all developments within your area of expertise, and for foster carers this means that there is a high expectation that you will attend training events and generally take every opportunity to increase your knowledge.

Obviously, while it is an important way to gain knowledge, attending training or completing online learning is not the only way in which you can do this. Reading articles in magazines and newspapers, watching documentaries on TV and listening to things on the radio are all valid ways to learn, but for many carers it is the discussions with other foster carers that really help their understanding, which is why training events and support groups are such a vital element of being a foster carer.

Furthermore, as a professional, it is not enough to just passively absorb information. There is a need for carers to actively challenge the information they hear to ensure that it has a sound evidential base and to understand the context in which the information is presented. Once again this is best achieved through attending training sessions where accredited trainers deliver the material or by undertaking e-learning from recognised providers...rather than just taking as gospel an article in some of our more salubrious tabloids!

So what will you need to learn?

This is a sensible question but not one that has an easy answer, as it may be influenced by what previous experiences you had before becoming a carer. It may be safe to assume that if you were a teacher previously you might be more aware of, say, child development, than had you been a plumber! But even that assumption might not be accurate if you were a plumber with lots of birth children or a teacher of just one age group! So basically, the learning needs of every carer will be unique and – almost – infinite!

However, there are, initially, some 'core' topics that every foster carer will need to know and, while this might vary from agency to agency and authority to authority, they include the following:

- *Child protection:* all carers need to have at least a basic knowledge of the legislation, an awareness of local policies and procedures, and an understanding of the types of abuse that children may have experienced.

- *Safe care:* as well as keeping the child safe it is necessary to ensure that carers also keep themselves safe. This may be safe from allegations or it may be safe from potentially unknown behaviours or emotional outbursts from the children in their care.

- *Valuing diversity:* the children and young people coming into care come from the full spectrum of families living in Britain, and it is important that carers have an awareness and acceptance, indeed an appreciation, of 'diversity' in all its forms.

- *First aid:* while first aid itself is important, there should ideally be training offered specifically for paediatric first aid.

- *Working with sexually abused children:* although it might not be known when a child is placed whether or not they have been sexually abused, all carers need to be prepared to discover that the child living with them may have been sexually abused in the past. Being forewarned means you are better prepared.

- *Attachment:* our understanding of how the brain develops and in particular how attachments are created and maintained, and the different styles of attachment, will help you to better understand what 'makes your child tick'.

- *De-escalation and restraint:* while the emphasis should clearly be on 'de-escalation', there needs to be training for all carers in respect of both this and, in case de-escalation fails, restraint – the latter being used rarely and predominantly to keep the child or young person safe from themselves.

- *Managing challenging behaviour:* many children will exhibit behaviours that are 'challenging'. This may be for a variety of reasons, but it is important that all carers have an awareness of how to manage these. Ideally this should be through a recognised, evidence-informed approach, such as the Fostering Changes programme devised by SLAM (South London and Maudsley Hospitals), that is used consistently with the child by all adults they come into contact with.

And what else?

In addition to this 'core' training that all carers will be expected to undertake (and periodically be asked to revisit in order to stay 'up to date'), there will be a whole range of training required.

This will vary depending on the needs of any child in placement and the skills, knowledge, experience and confidence of the carer. However, some key topics that I recommend attending training for include foetal alcohol spectrum disorders, resilience (both to learn how to encourage this in the young people but also for yourselves as carers!), bereavement and loss, working with other professionals, self-harming behaviours, recording as a foster carer, men in foster care and online safety, but in truth there are far too many to list here!

How much training do I have to do?

As I hope I have made clear, training and learning should not be seen as a chore, as something extra to do, but as an integral part of your task as a foster carer to keep yourself up to date and informed in order to be better prepared should the need ever come up with a child entrusted to your care.

As such there is no set amount of learning and training that is required, although it may be that some agencies or authorities stipulate an annual minimum amount that needs to be done.

When do I do all this?

Most agencies and authorities will provide classroom-based training courses with a training calendar being created that will, it is hoped, contain a good mix of interesting and required courses. These events are often popular as they create opportunities for carers to meet with others, and frequently more 'learning' is done over the mid-course cup of tea and chat than through the formal training!

However, we also recognise that, for many reasons, attending classroom training can be difficult for carers; it may be that you also have a full-time job, or you may live some way from the centre, or you may (indeed almost certainly will!) be required to do the school run morning and afternoon, and maybe no one else can be trusted to look after the child in your care. For all these reasons, most agencies and authorities will also offer, in addition to their classroom training, the chance to do some e-learning so that carers can access training in their own homes at a time to suit them.

Of course you are also, as a foster carer, setting an example and being a role model for the children in your care. If you see 'training' as a chore that has to be completed, then this will transmit to the child. If, however, you actively seek out learning opportunities, see it as a way of growing yourself personally and if you share that learning with others, then this too will be contagious. And what could be better and more of an example than sitting down with the kids as they do their homework and doing yours beside them?

The importance of foetal alcohol spectrum disorders (FASD)

There are numerous reasons why a child might misbehave or have problems managing their own behaviour.

Key to dealing with this is for the carer to understand where this behaviour might have come from. While there is much attention given to what a child may have experienced or witnessed since birth, which will obviously impact on their behaviour, a very common but seriously unrecognised issue is what may have happened to the child during the pregnancy and, in particular, the impact of a mother drinking alcohol.

When pregnant women drink, the alcohol – which is a neurotoxin – basically kills neurons (brain cells) and will impact on whichever neurons are active at that precise moment in time in the pregnancy. Consequently, *every* child's experience of pre-birth alcohol is going to be unique, and because of so many other variables (the strength, the amount and the frequency of alcohol being consumed; the mother's metabolism; the day of the pregnancy it is drunk, and so on) there is a wide variation in how alcohol affects children.

Since January 2016 the medical advice has been clear to expectant mothers that they should not drink during pregnancy, but before then the advice was unclear. Also, it needs to be appreciated that many women will not know they are pregnant until sometime into the pregnancy and may well be drinking in the very early stages, when damage can still be caused.

What is FASD?

More accurately this should be 'What are FASD?' as FASD stands for foetal alcohol spectrum disorders, with the emphasis on the plural! Consequently, you cannot say a child has FASD, nor can a child have a diagnosis of FASD, but rather that they are 'foetally affected' or that they are 'on the spectrum'.

The three main conditions on the foetal alcohol spectrum are:

- foetal alcohol syndrome (FAS)

- alcohol-related neurodevelopmental disorder (ARND)

- alcohol-related birth defects (ARBD).

FAS affects about 10% of the full number of foetally affected children, and this condition presents with clearly visible signs, primarily through facial features. These easily identifiable and diagnosable signs include a thin upper lip, a smooth philtrum (the 'groove' under your nose) and a smaller gap between the eyes. There will also be neurodevelopmental issues alongside these visible signs.

ARND, however, is far more common, with approximately 90% of foetally affected children being affected with this condition, which is very hard to diagnose. These children will look normal but their thinking, behaviour and emotions may all be impacted on by the alcohol and, unless this is picked up early, their actions – coupled with them looking normal – lead people to think that they are 'naughty' (or that their parents/carers are not very good), and very quickly this can become a self-fulfilling prophecy.

ARBD usually affects either internal organs or limbs and accounts for quite a small percentage of children. However, most children with ARBD will also have either FAS or ARND.

So how common are foetal alcohol spectrum disorders?

We all know that drinking by women of child-rearing age (especially the 18–24-year-old age group) has dramatically increased since the mid-1970s. Alcohol is more readily available, in supermarkets and other outlets, than it ever was and has actually become relatively cheaper. More alcohol is targeted at women, and the rise of 'drinking at home' along with the whole 'ladette' culture has meant that the numbers of children who are born with the 'pre-existing condition' of being foetally affected by alcohol has also risen. It is estimated that in the UK about 3% of all children are 'on the spectrum', although, as we do not collate the figures, this may in fact be an underestimate.

A large number of the children coming into care do so as a result of parents who misuse drugs, and alcohol is the most dangerous and has the greatest impact of any drug, and so it is acknowledged that the numbers of foetally affected children in the care system is undoubtedly much higher than in the normal population.

A recent small-scale survey (in Peterborough) found that while the figure for foetally affected children was 3.5% in the general population, for looked-after children it was actually 27%. There is no reason to suppose that these figures would not be similar everywhere.

What can be a problem for carers is that children are not automatically screened for FASD and often the information as to whether their mother drank during pregnancy is not available. Inevitably, therefore, we look at other potential explanations and implement interventions which may not work and will create extra frustration (for both carer and child), so it is vital that we explore whether the birth mum drank during pregnancy. If she did – as is very likely – then this might be a more plausible explanation for any behavioural or emotional issues the child presents.

So what behaviours can be expected?

As every foetally affected child will have been uniquely affected, there is no uniform set of behaviours that can be attributed to FASD. However, there are a few common 'themes' that can be identified:

- Much of the damage caused by alcohol concentrates on the frontal lobes where we have our 'executive functioning' located. This means that many of the children will have problems with memory, with the retrieval of information and with organisational skills.

- Many of these children will have issues with regulating their emotions, with very poor or limited ability to self-regulate, meaning that they have poor impulse control.

- A lot of foetally affected children also have a separate condition (where there is overlap with other neurodevelopmental conditions, this is referred to as 'co-morbidity') called sensory integration disorder, which means that they can be either hypersensitive or hyposensitive to a range of sensory experiences including smell, taste and touch.

- Many children on the spectrum struggle with abstract concepts such as maths, money and time, and will equally struggle with cause and effect, meaning that reward charts or star charts are generally not successful.

However, it bears repeating that every child's experience of alcohol will be unique, and consequently the impact on them will be unique.

So how can their behaviour be managed?
The first thing to say is that there is no 'cure' or solution to FASD. This is permanent brain damage that will last throughout their life. Instead we talk about 'strategies'.

The key strategy is for the carer to 'reframe' the child's behaviours given their understanding that they may have been caused by the mother's drinking pre-birth. This may sound easy, but it does require practice and patience!

Another key strategy is for the carer to become the child's 'external brain'! By this we mean that the alcohol has caused permanent brain damage and the carer needs to identify the aspects of the child's daily living that this has affected and then compensate for this by coming up with imaginative ideas and lateral thinking!

Many of these children will learn best in a visual way, so any lateral thinking and imaginative ideas that include visuals are most likely to succeed.

The best outcome, however, is for the carer to have an understanding and an appreciation that the behaviours, the actions and the thinking of the child has been compromised by a pre-existing condition and that it is not their fault. Once a carer can embrace this concept, then they will find it easier to identify the behaviour to manage.

Conclusion

As a foster carer you will always be learning. You will learn from every foster child you look after, you will learn from other foster carers, you will learn from other parents and you will learn through training.

Continually developing your skills by attending training is a vital part of being a good foster carer. It is absolutely vital that you seek out and continue to attend training. There is always new research into helping children recover from early trauma and neglect, new techniques and parenting approaches that might enable you to help your foster child to achieve their potential.

Alongside this, attending training allows you to catch up with other foster carers and their experiences, and often you will get as much from this as you will from the training that you are jointly doing.

Chapter 7

ALLEGATIONS – HOW TO HANDLE THEM AND WHAT TO EXPECT

—— Andy Elvin ——

Allegations of mistreatment are not regular or frequent in foster care but nor are they uncommon. It is important to be aware of this and to be aware of the process that follows an allegation that your foster child may make about you or your family. There is no disguising the fact that it is an unpleasant process. This chapter will take you through the process that follows an allegation and will provide case studies from foster carers who have been through this experience.

All foster carers receive training and guidance to help them provide a safe environment for the child and all members of the foster family. You should have received information about child protection and safeguarding procedures from your agency or local authority.

It is important that you record any incidents or complaints as they can provide important evidence if an allegation is made. You will be provided with incident sheets so that you can do this promptly, as well as recording in your daily diary.

If an allegation or complaint is made against you or your family, this can place you in a difficult and sometimes distressing situation. If the allegation is made directly to a social worker they have a responsibility to make you aware of it. You will be allocated an independent person to support you through any investigation, as your supervising social worker may be required to give evidence which is not in support of you.

There are ways in which you can reduce risks of allegations or complaints being made:

- Think about who in the household may be vulnerable to allegations.

- Keep a daily record and maintain your diary.

- Be clear on what behaviour is expected.

- Develop your own safer caring policy for keeping everyone safe.

- Make use of training and support from your supervising social worker.

- Have insurance cover – this is provided through your membership of The Fostering Network or Foster Talk.

- Work closely with other professionals and talk to them about any concerns you have.

What happens if an allegation is made?

If an allegation is made it will be investigated fairly and confidentially and the local safeguarding children board procedures will be followed.

A strategy meeting will be called within two working days of the allegation to decide whether an investigation is necessary and whether your own children should be considered as part of a child protection conference. This is a meeting of child protection social workers from the local authority, the police child protection team and other relevant professionals in the case.

Where appropriate you will be given the chance to respond to the allegation before a final decision is made about what action to take.

The minutes of this meeting and any relevant information will be held on your record. In some situations, the local authority may look for a new placement for the child and a decision may be made to not place any other children with you during the investigation and until there is an outcome to the investigation.

If an allegation is made against you, you will be notified verbally and in writing.

Your supervising social worker will not be able to discuss the allegation during the investigation. Your agency will inform you of:

- how you will be supported while you are under investigation

- the address and contact telephone number of an independent person who will provide you with support during the investigation

- details of the support you can access from The Fostering Network

- information regarding a solicitor if you need this

- information on insurance arrangements for legal expenses.

A foster child might make a false allegation of abuse:

- because of misinterpreting an innocent action

- to bring attention to previous abuse for the first time because you or someone in the household is trusted

- as a way to have some control over their life which may seem out of control

- to bring an end to a foster placement.

The outcome of the investigation may:

- identify training or support needs for you
- require consideration of your approval category at your annual review
- recommend a return to the fostering panel for further discussion
- recommend that you are no longer suitable to foster.

If an allegation is made directly to you about another person's behaviour towards a child, you should inform your supervising social worker or the child's social worker as soon as possible or within 24 hours.

CASE STUDY

We were aware that the 14-year-old placed with us had made allegations against her previous carers. We also knew that she was very young emotionally. She was very single minded and found it very difficult to see anyone's point of view but her own. She was a bully at school but stood up for her friends, often getting involved and getting into trouble when it was nothing to do with her.

She was told by other children in care that she was entitled to have her own flat at 16 despite everyone in the professional network explaining to her that it wasn't going to happen.

When she was 17 there was an incident where she used her size and weight to try and intimidate me. After the incident we were a bit shaken because we hadn't done anything and there had been no build up to it. I was glad she hadn't kicked off when either of us was alone with her.

I was always the one who made the rules; my husband was the one who took her to football, guides and college when she needed a lift. So for her to then make an allegation against my husband, as she did, was hard for him.

All support from our agency and social services in terms of discussing the allegation was gone, and the only thing we could do was to phone The Fostering Network helpline. Though we were aware that this is what would happen, it was hard.

Our fostering agency was reassuring and supportive and came with me to the police interview with my husband. The policeman didn't feel the need to come out to interview me – it was done over the phone.

No one tells you what's happening, and people you talk to weekly suddenly don't ring. We had months of not knowing what was happening. We were confident we had done nothing wrong and supported each other. We don't need to foster; we choose to foster.

The Police decided there was nothing to substantiate the allegation so the investigation was closed. The positive thing was that a child in placement was not removed, which indicated that, although they couldn't say anything, no one believed she was in danger.

I have met up with her and she rings me every now and then. We have no hard feelings and wish her the best.

CASE STUDY

When I first started my fostering journey, just after completing my Skills to Foster course, I was full of excitement and looking forward to receiving my first placement and keeping in touch with the friends I had made on the course.

Three months later I had a call from my fostering agency asking me if I was happy to offer a placement to two unaccompanied minors, one of whom later became a selective mute. It all started wonderfully, with the children seemingly enjoying their new lives, starting at a local school, getting on and enjoying their school and homework, as well as regular day trips, including a visit to a festival in London. All in all they were a polite couple of teenagers with whom I quickly built what I thought was a strong relationship.

To help them move on from their terrible pasts, they were both offered therapy, which I cheerfully encouraged in order to allow the young boy who was a selective mute to come out of his shell a little. They started their therapy, and apart from the occasional times I checked to see if they still enjoyed it, I thought nothing more of it.

Then, one day, I received a telephone call from my social worker cancelling the supervision session, then another from my social worker's manager, saying that an allegation had been made against me. I was reminded that I was entitled to support and advice from The Fostering Network and encouraged to contact them. I quickly remembered my Skills to Foster training and how I thought I would never be in this situation. I'd never inappropriately touch or affect a child's life!

A few hours later I had the police knocking on the door, asking if they could speak to me. After some questions they informed me that I was being cautioned, to which I replied, 'Does that mean I'm under arrest?' Words cannot describe the fear and sickness I felt when I was speaking to the officer. I was completely innocent, confused and terrified all at the same time!

Thankfully, I always kept my logs completely up to date, and after the police officer had checked them and questioned me, he was happy to allow the children to return home that night from school.

It turns out that, during therapy, the young boy had made some hand gestures that were interpreted as an indication that I had hit him! I was outraged to say the least!

To make matters worse, I had planned a nice trip to a Will Young concert that evening and had to spend time alone with him, which I felt uncomfortable doing, but tried to keep the placement as normal as possible. This had a profound effect on my children, who were extremely worried about my well-being. Although my fostering agency offered me support, I still felt helpless and alone, and I was scared of sharing my situation with anyone else in case they unfairly judged me or the children.

I then had to go through the process of waiting for the investigation to be finished by the police, fostering agency and the LADO (Local Authority Diagnosed Officer). After eight weeks of investigation I was found to have done no wrong. The children were eventually moved closer to some family members in the country. I then went to the fostering panel and was reapproved to continue my career as a foster carer.

All in all, although it was a huge emotional stress to me and my family, I feel that I learned a lot from the situation, and to this day I always keep my logs up to date!

CASE STUDY

In the summer of 2015 we took our three foster children aged 12, 14 and 17 and our birth daughter C, who was 24, on holiday to Greece. We had been experiencing problems with the young girl who was 17 since May of that year, where she would stay out all night without permission, and was drinking, smoking and using drugs. In fact, she had gone missing the evening prior to us going away.

While we were at the resort the girl had refused to come back to the accommodation until the early hours of the morning and kept one of the younger children out on one occasion until 3am.

The three young people were missing one evening from the hotel. C and myself were searching for them for about an hour and a half. We eventually found them at about 11pm. The 17-year-old accused C of hitting her.

On our return to the UK we gave 28 days' notice on the placement of the 17-year-old on the grounds that she had refused to follow any of our rules and boundaries, which made it impossible for us to keep her safe. The following day the young person made a formal complaint to my supervising social worker that my daughter C had been physically and verbally abusive to her.

Immediately the supervising social worker was unable to discuss anything with me. C was asked to stay at her boyfriend's until the matter could be investigated. She was extremely upset and very unhappy about being asked to leave the family home. C has always depended on us for support in difficult times and found it extremely difficult being the one asked to leave, when in her eyes she had done no wrong and was being wrongly accused.

TACT advised us that we were entitled to support from The Fostering Network and arranged for us to have an independent support worker.

TACT conducted a full risk assessment, as the other children in our care were from a different local authority and social care needed to know that it was safe for them to remain in the placement.

The girl who made the allegation remained in our care for a further ten days. This was a difficult time for us and for C, who couldn't return home until the young person had left, and she was unable to be left unsupervised around the other young people for a number of months.

Although originally the young people had stated that they hadn't seen the alleged assault, they later told their social worker that they had. One of them said that she was frightened of C and wanted to be moved from the placement; they had been with us for over two years at this point. I felt that the young person was unsure of her feelings due to experiences in her past. This made decision making difficult for her. Things settled down after a few months, and I am happy to say that the young people have now been with us for almost four years and are happy and doing well.

The risk assessment conducted by TACT using the Signs of Safety model concluded that on a scale of 0–10 – 10 being that the placement is completely safe – we were awarded a score of 9. The local authority agreed with this outcome.

I feel that although the risk assessment was a difficult process it gives us protection for the future, as further allegations surrounding this incident cannot be revisited.

My husband and I found the whole process of the allegation emotionally draining. We felt that we had little control of our normal lives, with C being asked to leave the family home and the placement of the other two young people being in jeopardy.

This isn't something that we would like to experience again in the future but feel that due to good recording and the very thorough risk assessment the outcome was good.

Conclusion

Allegations are a fact of life when working with vulnerable children and adults. Do not spend your whole time as a foster carer walking on eggshells in order to try and avoid an allegation, because they are not frequent or common. Making sure that your recording is up to date, having a good and up-to-date safer caring policy and sharing any issues that are troubling you with your social worker are all important in maintaining a foster home that is safe for all of you. The process of investigating an allegation is stressful and can feel very lonely. You have the right support, so do access this and be prepared to challenge if you think that the situation is dragging on.

As one foster carer says:

'Our experience with allegations was a long process, very frustrating and time consuming. Trying to understand the procedures was difficult, as it can take up to a year for everything to be resolved, based on whether the child comes from the local borough or out of borough and also depending on the nature of the allegations. We had a long and difficult time; although one of us was working it still makes it difficult when there is no income for the other partner. There is a lot of waiting for everything to be resolved, and then after it is all sorted out, there is a wait to find another placement. We felt that although support from our agency was there, it did not make our lives any easier. We never gave up on fostering and never planned to. We came into this to make a better life for the children; it's not easy, but it is well worth it once they move on and they have a better view on life. I do feel that the procedures could be shortened somehow. To have to wait so long to get allegations sorted, even when they are false, does not make things any easier.'

Above all, please don't let an allegation end your fostering career. Many excellent foster carers have had allegations made against them, but have come through it and continued to offer exemplary care to vulnerable children.

Chapter **8**

MANAGING CONTACT

Martin Barrow and Andy Elvin

Contact between your foster child and their birth family is extremely important. It can be vital for your child to maintain contact with their parents and relatives. It is beholden on foster carers to promote this contact and to speak positively to their foster children about their birth family.

Contact is one of the most emotional aspects of foster care – arranging for children and their families from whom they are separated to keep in touch with one another. The management of contact is one of the toughest aspects of fostering.

Depending on what sort of placement you have, you might find that you are managing a lot of contact. For example, if you are looking after a very young child or baby and their case is still in care proceedings, then you may find that you are managing contact on a daily basis. This is because the court will not prejudice the outcome of the final hearing; if the child is not living with their birth parent the court will make sure that the child has regular contact to maintain the relationship because they may be returning home. Therefore, if you are seeking to foster very young children and babies, you must be prepared for the fact that you will be managing a high level of contact.

If court proceedings have ended and it has been decided the child will be remaining with you long term, the level of contact may not be so high but it may be equally important. In such a long-term arrangement you may well find yourself managing the contact more and more and making the arrangements with the birth family.

Children who are taken into foster care generally maintain contact with their birth families. The level of contact varies from placement to placement, according to a number of factors. The reasons for the intervention will be taken into account, as will any potential risk to the child.

Current practice assumes a strong underlying principle, supported by legislation, that contact is generally beneficial and should be promoted as long as it is in the child's best interests and does not increase risk. Significant resources are committed to supporting contact, which can be a positive experience for children and their birth families and help build the foundations for a better future as parents work to overcome their troubles.

The relationship between you and the birth family can sometimes be a difficult one and may, at times, feel burdensome. It is important to try and empathise with how the birth parents and the wider birth family are feeling about the situation and to approach communication with them with that very much in mind. You are looking after their child; you have been chosen to care for their child whom they have been told, possibly by the courts, they cannot safely look after. Stop and think about this for a few minutes. How would you feel if you were in their situation? Also think about the importance to the child of maintaining these relationships and making them as positive as they can possibly be.

A conflictual relationship between you and the birth family is likely to be very difficult for the child if they want to maintain contact with their birth family. You may therefore find yourself holding your breath and counting to ten on a number of occasions, but it is important that you try, as much as possible, to think of the situation from the point of view of the child's parents or relatives. Your priority must always be the child – the child's wishes and feelings, and how to make contact as positive as possible for the child.

A good contact session should leave the child feeling reassured that they are loved and missed by their parents and still belong to them. They will have heard about what has been going on in their family in detail and the bonds will be kept alive. It is particularly important, where appropriate, that children from a dual heritage background, or who are not a cultural match but are placed with you, maintain their links with their family, friends and community so that their cultural history is encouraged, developed and valued.

At its best, contact helps maintain and even strengthen the relationship between parent and child. It helps a foster child to see that a parent is doing well, or taking positive steps towards reuniting the family. During an extended placement, regular parental contact can reinforce a child's sense of identity. It gives parents hope that there can be a bright future beyond the current difficulties, and reassurance that their child is being well cared for. When their capacity as parents is still being assessed, it is important for them to have the opportunity to demonstrate how they relate to their children.

However, contact can also cause distress to the children and set back the progress that they have made in care. Frequently there is tension between lofty aspirations of parental contact and the reality. Children may have ambivalent feelings towards meeting with their parents, wanting it, but feeling distressed at the same time. This is often the case with children who are old enough to understand the reasons why they are in care and to articulate their sense of anger. Parents can also be angry, still contesting the reasons for the intervention of social services and resentful of the restrictions imposed on them. They sometimes take it out on the children, or even reject them. Seeing the children doing well can, in itself, be a source of frustration and anger.

High-frequency contact for infants (for example, four to seven times a week) can be particularly problematic and distressing, causing disruption to their daily routines and making it difficult for them to experience settled caregiving.

As a foster carer, you have a critical role in judging what is best for your foster child. You will listen to the child's concerns and work with the fostering team to agree the appropriate level of contact. This is likely to change during the course of the placement and may even vary from week to week. At times you may come under pressure for your foster child to attend a contact session that you feel is not right. It is important for you to express your concerns, and if you do not receive a satisfactory answer, to refuse to allow the child to attend the session. As always, trust your judgement.

Arrangements for contact visits will be made at the planning meeting at the start of the placement and a schedule will be shared with all interested parties. Make sure that these arrangements are appropriate for your foster child, taking into account things like schooling and the travelling distance to contact sessions. Also, make sure that they work for you and your family. Everything should be written down so that all those involved are clear about what has been agreed, but be explicit about the need to keep these arrangements under review, according to the child's needs. For example, children of school age will attend contact after a long day in the classroom, and with homework still to be done. Sometimes, it is just too much.

Contact sessions take several forms; again, this will be determined by the nature of the placement, the needs of the children and the capacity of the parents. Typically, the session will take place in a dedicated family contact centre, or in a council-owned building often attached to a public library or civic centre. Alternatively, parents may be allowed to take their children into the community, perhaps to a park or a restaurant.

Contact is most likely to be overseen by a family contact supervisor, who will have experience in working with children and families. The contact supervisor's general role is to provide assistance, support and encouragement to foster carers, as well as foster children and their birth families. The contact supervisor also makes sure that parents abide by any pre-agreed conditions imposed on the session. Conditions are likely to include topics of conversation (such as discussion about allegations made against them, or criticism of the foster carers), use of a language other than English, sharing of mobile devices, and the type of food and drink that can be given to the child. Some children's services have a contract that birth parents are required to sign.

However, the contact supervisor's scope to facilitate a good contact session may be inhibited by the purpose of the session. For example, if a parent is being assessed to help the family court reach a decision about a child's long-term future, the contact supervisor must use discretion in allowing a parent to interact with the child, intervening only when the child becomes visibly upset. Equally, the contact supervisor sometimes must decide whether the child wants the session to be brought to an end, even though the child has not explicitly asked for this, either because they don't have the language to do so or through fear of upsetting the parent.

The contact supervisor usually collects the foster child from the foster home or school and takes them to the contact session. Sometimes the foster carer is tasked with taking the foster child to and from the contact session. This should be agreed in advance at the placement planning meeting, and not become an ad-hoc arrangement to cover for an absent or late-running contact supervisor. The contact supervisor writes a report for the fostering team after each contact session, which is used to monitor changes in the relationship between birth parents and their children.

A good contact supervisor is worth their weight in gold. It is a difficult role, but one that is central to a successful outcome of a fostering placement. Some local authorities underestimate its importance and use a number of supervisors with little regard for the impact of this constant change on vulnerable children.

Your foster child may spend several hours a week with the contact supervisor, in their car and in the contact session, and they will be together at times of emotional turmoil. The contact session can be less stressful for the child if there is another familiar face in the room, and a person who really understands how they feel. A regular, experienced contact supervisor can spot signs of stress and guide conversations towards calmer waters. There is an additional complexity when contact takes place in a public setting, such as a restaurant or park, and is witnessed by other people, so a child is likely to be reassured if they know and trust the contact supervisor.

Local agencies develop close working relationships with contact supervisors. Their feedback after contact sessions is invaluable in helping to understand and manage foster children's anxieties about their birth families. Although time is always at a premium, it is important for them to have a chat about the children when they return home and share thoughts about the best way to address any concerns. In some placements, the contact supervisor is one of very few people to get to know the children and understand what they are living through. They can be effective advocates for them, and for you as a foster carer.

Foster carers can agree to take children to contact sessions, although they rarely act as supervisors. Often, foster carers take responsibility for transporting the very youngest children (typically, babies or pre-schoolers), but a contact supervisor transports older children. This represents a significant commitment of time, but can be less disruptive for children, which, in turn, is beneficial for the placement.

Taking children to contact sessions is likely to bring you into contact with members of the birth family, which can be a challenge as well as an opportunity. Many contact centres do not have separate entrances and exits to facilitate separate comings and goings for birth families and carers. There is a potential risk of confrontation, although generally this is rare. Undoubtedly it is difficult for parents to see their children arrive and leave in the care of another family, and it's important to mitigate the impact. For example, goodbyes can be said to the children in the car, out of their parents' view, and the handover can be completed as quickly as possible, at least in the early stages of the placement.

Over time, these encounters with the parents two or three times a week can develop into a more positive relationship, to the benefit of the foster children. Sometimes other family members, particularly grandparents, act as a bridge. Engaging a grandparent in brief, polite conversation, then maybe an aunt or a sister, can lead in due course to one or both parents becoming involved. It takes time to win trust, and sometimes there are setbacks. But it is possible to build a relationship with birth parents. It certainly does the children a power of good to see their parents in polite conversation with their foster carers.

What's more, some of the relationships forged outside a contact centre can develop into friendships, which have helped foster carers to remain in contact with foster children after they have moved on.

For children in care, parental contact sessions can be an emotional and exhausting experience. As a foster carer, you will spend a significant amount of time and energy dealing with the fallout from contact sessions that have gone awry. A common problem is that parents fail to show up for the session. There are many reasons for this. It may be as a result of a breakdown in communication with social workers, or difficulty in getting time off work. Or it could be further evidence of an erratic lifestyle, or a failure to prioritise children over other commitments. Whatever the reason, it causes immense distress to a child who may have been anxious or excited about spending time with a parent but now feels utterly rejected.

There is a risk that contact sessions become an opportunity for parents to vent their frustration about care proceedings. Instead of focusing on the children and encouraging them to talk about what they have been doing, parents become increasingly agitated and turn the session into a rant. This can deepen a child's feelings of guilt and helplessness.

Contact sessions are particularly complex when sibling groups are involved. Siblings will respond in different ways to the situation in which they find themselves, and may compete among themselves for their parents' attention. In turn, parents may appear to favour a child who is sympathetic, and shun a sibling who blames them for what happened. This creates further tension between siblings, who bring their anxieties home with them to their foster carers.

Gifts from parents often become the focal point of contact sessions. It is not uncommon for parents to seek to compensate for their absence by buying increasingly lavish presents (which they can usually ill afford). This encourages children to treat contact as a competition to secure the best presents. Any hope of creating a strong family bond through the contact sessions is lost.

Often, the longer the foster placement continues, the greater the strain on arrangements for parental contact. The emotional burden on the children is not sustainable. When siblings are involved, their expectations of contact diverge. There are competing demands on their time, such as after-school activities and social events with new friends. By now, they are making unfavourable comparisons between their birth families and their foster carers, or their friends' families. The children themselves often ask if they can skip contact to do something else, or the number of contact sessions can be reduced. Sometimes this is what they want, but are afraid to ask.

The stress of parental contact can have a detrimental impact on a foster child's behaviour, and cause mood swings. Some children become subdued or disruptive as they mentally prepare themselves to meet a parent, and take time to settle afterwards. It can affect their appetite, and you should be alert to the increased risk to children with a history of self-harm. You may feel that the good work you have done over, say, a weekend to restore calm and rebuild confidence is then laid to waste by a bad contact session.

Your role as foster carer is to help your foster child navigate through the minefield that is parental contact. Often you stand alone between the child and the competing interests of birth parents, social workers and lawyers. At times, you may feel that social workers put the needs of birth parents ahead of the children's needs.

Sometimes your job is to do nothing other than listen to the child as they try to process conflicting emotions. But a child will also look to you for answers, which you may not be able to give.

In order to protect your child's best interests, it is essential for you to document the impact of parental contact, including the positives and the negatives. Information about parental contact sessions should form a significant part of your diary notes. Be precise in noting changes in behaviour, and in reporting what your foster child tells you about how they are feeling, even if what they say is contradictory. Ask the questions about contact without leading them one way or another. Try to keep an open mind, even if your instinct is to respond quickly by demanding changes to contact arrangements. Give the child time to reflect and talk things through again the next day, when the situation may be calmer.

Work closely with the child's social worker. Sometimes contact sessions can be improved simply by changing venue or times, or providing additional support to parents who may be struggling to cope. Encourage your child to take along something to play with, such as a game or a colouring book. It may be something that a parent could join in with. Food may be a concern – try giving your foster child a healthy snack before they leave for contact, which will discourage them from gorging on unhealthy food provided by the parents. Make it absolutely clear to the child that he or she can terminate the contact at any time, without fear of criticism. Maybe you could even agree a signal for the child and the contact supervisor to use when the child wants to leave.

Sometimes foster carers are given a contact book for exchanging information with the birth family. This is most likely to be used in the case of infants or toddlers. Where young children are having very regular contact with their birth family, early in proceedings, say three or four times a week, the contact book becomes a line of communication between you to ensure that the child receives consistent care. Sometimes due to travel arrangements or particular issues, foster carers will not see the birth family, and information about diet, routines, likes and dislikes are best written down. For example, carers can write in the contact book the time a baby was fed and changed, whether all the milk was taken, or perhaps request that the cream for nappy rash is applied. Often in this situation it is best to also note down any bumps or scrapes the child may have acquired in play or by accident, with a short explanation of what happened. This can avoid misunderstandings and anxiety. If the health visitor has seen the child at your home, it is helpful to record this in the contact book and share with parents the comments about the child's progress, including weight gain. Also for small children, developments and new abilities should be noted and shared with the birth family via the contact book.

Over time, these brief, factual notes can evolve into something more engaging, particularly if you meet occasionally at the beginning and end of contact sessions. Don't expect too much, but a kind word from you in the margin of information about nappies and feeding can mean a lot to a parent struggling to come to terms with what has happened.

Conclusion

Parental contact can be the most challenging aspect of foster care. It is important to remember that the responsibility for making contact work in the best interests of children should be shared with the contact supervisor, social workers and, above all, the birth family. Always share your concerns, and make sure you can back these up with dates and times of incidents and issues that have caused distress. Never go along with arrangements that make you feel uncomfortable.

Talk to other foster carers about your worries. It will help you to know that they are dealing with similar issues. They may also have good practical advice, based on their knowledge of the same contact centre or contact supervisor.

None of this is to say that you should support negative contact or not raise concerns if you genuinely feel that the contact is detrimental to the child's welfare. If you are aware of anything that happens during contact that places the child's welfare at risk, you must immediately inform your supervising social worker, likewise if your foster child's behaviour before and after contact is concerning you.

Contact with the birth family is important and must be promoted as far as possible; sometimes this will be challenging and sometimes it will be extremely positive. Children's relationships with their birth parents and with siblings can be complicated but they will be lifelong, so it is important to positively support them whenever possible.

Chapter 9

THE BIRTH PARENTS' PERSPECTIVE

—— A safeguarding survivor ——

I write this as a birth mum whose family has had years of experience of the child protection system. I have voluntarily placed some of my children into foster care on several occasions when my mental health has been in crisis. On the last of those occasions, my local authority, quite rightly, issued care proceedings to ensure that my children did not experience any further disruption. I recognised the local authority's concerns and began to make significant changes to my life. However, being pregnant during those proceedings, my newborn baby was removed at six days old and placed, against my will, into foster care with an ultimate plan of non-consensual adoption. I continued to make changes to my life, sustained those changes and contested the case. My son came home to me 258 days after he had been taken and has remained in my care since then. I have three children at home with me, and three still in the care system with foster carers. In my own personal experience, and the experience I now have of supporting parents of looked-after children through my work relationships with foster carers can be complex.

As birth parents, we can feel immensely grateful to you for looking after our children when we cannot. We can recognise the value you are bringing to our children's lives, the time that you spend with them, the attention you give them and the truly wonderful, selfless way in which you open your homes and hearts. We can feel relief that there exists such a 'safety net' in this country, and an odd sense of security in the knowledge that our children are being looked after by someone who has been trained to do so. We can also get attached to you – after all, you have our children, so how could we not?

However, we can also feel immensely resentful towards you for all the same reasons. We can feel a deep and painful jealousy; that time you spend with our children, that attention you shower on them, that should be our time and our attention. We can feel suspicious of your motives for fostering, and we can feel you have 'stolen' our children. We can feel insecure about our own parenting, that you do it better, and that may cause us to pick faults with you or your home or your own family. We can feel fear that our children prefer you and may not wish to come home to us. We can feel that we are 'competing' with you, and this is further exacerbated when it comes to things like Christmas and birthdays. We can feel a real and palpable hatred for you, especially when we think about you cuddling our children or sharing any sort of bond with them.

My experiences have been a bit of everything, all intertwined with a deep-seated guilt for failing my children in the first instance. It takes courage from the very depths of our soul to allow ourselves to identify the positives foster carers bring to our children's lives. It is not an easy task. I now spend a great deal of time writing my blog and talking to birth parents to try to help them get to that point. But there are things you, as foster carers, can do to help:

- Remain, at all times, respectful of the birth parents' role and recognise that we are, in most cases, the experts on our children's lives. Whether the plan for the children is a rehabilitation home, special guardianship, long-term fostering or adoption, we are always still their birth parents. It might be all we have to cling to at times.

- Use our expertise to help you in your role. If we as birth parents are treated in this way, we are far more likely to engage with not only you, but also the local authority as a whole. We might have a particular style of parenting or have a particular routine our children follow. Things that are important to us and that our children are used to, like the gentle parenting approach or a baby wearing cloth nappies, may not be familiar to you, but it would have such a positive effect on our relationship if you were to research them, or even try them.

- Support breastfeeding however you can. This is tremendously important if you have our newborn or young babies. When you are separated from your child at birth, or soon after, breastfeeding is all you can give that child. It's something you can do for them that nobody else can. I cannot stress enough how valuable it is to have a foster carer who understands this and supports the mother with this. It may be arranging to collect breastmilk from the mother, or that she can bring milk to contact sessions, but however it is done, your role is key.

- Be aware of special family occasions and promote good contact. One of our foster carers always ensures that my children send their siblings (and me!) birthday cards. This helps so much in terms of relationship building between family members – as well as between you and the birth parents – and can help to break down barriers.

- Be mindful of the importance of our family connection. The time you are spending with our children is time we are not. We don't know what our children are doing when they are with you, and this alone can be very difficult. I remember looking outside at the sky and knowing my children were under it – but that was all I knew. As such, being given photographs of activities can be very welcome. Conversely, it can also feel a bit like your nose is being rubbed in it – so do ask the birth parent if it is something they would like! Other things – such as ensuring that we know when parents' evenings are at school, or if our children have assemblies or performances – are also very important to our family.

- Contact can be a very emotional time for the whole family. It is sometimes very difficult for parents to engage in contact, particularly under supervised conditions. Imagine if someone was watching you, in an artificial environment, using a notepad to record your every move. It isn't easy, and although I struggled through it, some parents don't have the strength that I did. I can't bear the thought of any child left waiting at contact for parents who don't show up, but I do understand why some can't commit to it. I don't think there's much you can do other than to try to understand, too. The vast majority of parents don't want to hurt their children and don't want to let them down, but it's not always as simple as that.

- Keep in touch, when you can. If a child returns home, many parents simply want to concentrate on looking after their family themselves and moving on from an awful period in their lives. Others, however, will want to keep in touch with you, in whatever way possible, and I'd hope that that would be reciprocated. My youngest son's foster carers are part of his jigsaw. When he came home, his foster mum sent me a text to say, 'Your son is coming home to you, where he belongs.' She and her husband sent gifts and cards to us all and they are in his memory box for when he is older. He has met them once since he's been home, although he has no memory of them. I think it is tremendously important that he is able to meet them again when he's older, if he chooses to. I will certainly always be grateful to them. They gave him the love, care and attention I was not, for reasons beyond my control, able to. Fostering is truly a wonderful thing.

Chapter **10**

WORKING WITH THE PROFESSIONAL NETWORK

Yvonne Smith, Jon Fayle and Andy Elvin

As a foster carer you will find yourself working with a range of professionals to support your foster child. In this chapter, one of TACT's foster carer representatives gives her perspective on working with the professional network, and an independent reviewing officer talks about his work.

Working with your professional network – Yvonne Smith

Working effectively with the professional network can greatly assist in achieving good outcomes for your foster child. Sometimes you may find it frustrating and feel that you are excluded from meetings or decisions. Never be afraid to advocate for your foster child or to, politely, raise with the professional network that you are the one who is caring for the child on a daily basis and, other than the birth parents, you are the person who knows the child best. Too often, the views and input of foster carers are overlooked by those in the professional network. It should be very rare that important meetings making decisions about your foster child are held without you being present.

Though you may not consider yourself an expert or a professional in the same way as a teacher, doctor, mental health worker or social worker, you are the expert on your foster child. Decisions made without your input are likely to be poorer and less informed than those made with you as an active part of the discussion and decision-making process.

The role of the foster carer, when engaging with other professionals within the inter-agency framework, varies according to local circumstances. However, all practice must be guided by both local and national frameworks and policies. The policies set out the standards of ethical practice that provide clarity and protection for all involved. Therefore, a foster carer working within the professional network depends on good interpersonal skills and the knowledge of the appropriate legal and policy frameworks that the other professionals will be working from. It is also a good idea to establish who is responsible for the date and timing of any meetings held and who will be taking the lead; for example, will it be the person who has called the meeting, will it be the same person who is taking the minutes or will the role be assumed by someone else?

It is vitally important that foster carers are involved in the planning and decision making for the child in their care. Their primary role is to take care of and be the voice of the child they have been entrusted with, to make quality judgements and promote the child's rights while being transparent and honest with other professionals. They are fundamental in creating a positive working environment with professional values.

The need to maintain professionalism in the face of challenging circumstances is paramount in order for the foster carer to be able to raise and address issues in relation to the child in their care. The foster carer needs to be confident to engage in effective collaboration with other professionals including social workers, teachers, health professionals and counsellors who may or may not be part of child and adolescent mental health services.

The foster carer will promote the child's best interests during any meeting, ensuring that the rights of the child are upheld. This is where an individual's empathy can help.

If a person possesses empathy, they can engage with the other professionals on the basis that they can see their priorities and points of view, which can differ to varying degrees. Empathy is a learned skill that can be used to understand situations and communicate effectively with other individuals.

Additionally, a foster carer needs to have the ability to engage people in both a knowledgeable and effective manner in order to establish the best possible outcome for the child in their care from any meeting held. There are a number of good working examples of this.

Once, when a local authority social worker came to transport a three-year-old from my home to a contact session, which was 13 miles away, the child was put on the back seat without a car seat being used. I was a little apprehensive about challenging this unlawful and ultimately unsafe practice because he was the social worker and I had only recently become a foster carer. However, I knew that I was the voice of the child and therefore insisted that a car seat be used, and I provided one for him. On their return, the child had been transported without sitting on the car seat. When I made a comment about it, the social worker told me that it was all right because she was in the middle seat in the back of the car; however, I disagreed with this statement. I raised the concern of poor practice with my local agency and the matter was dealt with accordingly. At all times, I acted in a professional manner by using the correct procedure to appropriately challenge the unsafe and unlawful practice by another professional in regard to a child in my care. To make sure there was a paper trail that could be followed, I logged it in my notes straightaway. With regards to meetings within the professional network, everything should be clearly recorded and reported where necessary.

Another example of effectively challenging a more senior professional arose when a child I was caring for was deemed to need therapy by the child's local authority social worker. I disagreed that it was in the child's best interests and took the initiative to speak to the child psychologist and the guardian involved with the child. After examining all the evidence available, we had a lengthy discussion about what the issues were deemed to be. Both the child psychologist and the guardian agreed with me that it was not in the child's best interests to undergo therapy. As a result, we were able to ensure that the child's needs were fully evaluated and met, and this did not include the need for therapy. Since then I have undertaken an NCFE Level 2 course in Awareness of Mental Health Problems, so that if a similar occasion were to occur I would be better placed to reinforce my understanding of the matter. Consequently, I would have no hesitation informing the health professionals that I understood the issues, as I have a relevant qualification in the subject, and furthermore I would be able to demonstrate my level of knowledge.

Another way to engage pro-actively with other professionals is in regard to education and school. A foster carer attends a child's personal education plan meeting at their school to discuss progress made by the child and how pupil premium funding will be used to further this progress. There may be times when the school refuses to allow the pupil premium to be used in a way that will advantage the child, if they have no extra educational needs in other ways. It is then the foster carer's responsibility to ensure that the money is spent on the child in their care for the best possible outcome for the child. This means that the funding can be used on emotional well-being as well as education-based resources. If required, they can take along a document in which the Department for Education (DfE) clearly states that the pupil premium can be used for 'helping adopted/looked-after children emotionally, socially and educationally by providing specific support to raise their attainment and address their wider needs'. This can be downloaded and printed from the government's website. Make sure to print enough copies for all professionals who will be attending the meeting.

I myself have challenged a school on this issue, with the correct DfE paperwork prepared and given to the other professionals to read during the meeting. If I had just gone in and said that I wanted swimming lessons to aid with the child's aqua phobia, which would benefit the child emotionally, the other professionals would have responded negatively because it was not educational. However, because I provided the appropriate evidence that what I was asking for was not unreasonable and was well within the scope of what is permitted within pupil premium funds, and then explained my reasoning for asking for swimming lessons, the other professionals at the meeting listened to what I had to say on behalf of the child. In this instance, for the child in my care, the school has paid for an after-school dance club on a weekly basis as well as out-of-school activities including swimming and guitar lessons. This is all to aid emotional well-being and social inclusion.

It is having the knowledge and taking the responsibility to use that knowledge which provides the confidence and understanding needed for a foster carer to successfully challenge colleagues and senior staff in a professional manner.

In conclusion, being able to successfully engage with other professionals is a skill that should be developed by all foster carers. Every foster carer should understand their role and the ethical duties that come with the position, and take the responsibility to do the best they can for the children in their care, even if it means challenging other professionals.

Nonetheless, challenging other professionals needs to be done in a confident, respectful manner, using the legal framework and policy that apply to the given situation. Using documented evidence whenever possible, and always making sure to use the correct channels, will maintain your own professionalism.

Furthermore, good verbal communication, effective speaking and active listening, as well as understanding your own identity and role as a foster carer while at the same time gaining an understanding of other professional roles, will effectively establish a network where mutual trust, respect and understanding lead to a collaborative approach. Only then will there be support for the best decisions and outcomes for the child in your care.

This then leads to a collaborative and co-ordinated approach to shared decision making, taking into account the differing needs of each professional body and resulting in social inclusion and equality for everyone concerned.

The role of the independent reviewing officer – Jon Fayle

As a foster carer, one of the key professionals that you will work with is the independent reviewing officer (IRO). A relatively new role, the IRO is responsible for scrutinising the child's care plan from an independent point of view and conducting periodic formal reviews of the child's case. A key responsibility of the IRO is to listen to the child carefully, to make sure the child's voice is heard strongly and effectively in the reviewing process, and to challenge the local authority if they believe it is necessary in the interest of the child. In this section I will:

- examine the background to the development of the IRO role

- describe the main components of the IRO role

- make some comments about the current IRO scene

- summarise research and other commentary on the performance and effectiveness of IROs since their introduction

- examine and explore good practice in relation to foster carers working with IROs.

Background

The importance of reviewing the progress of children in care in a formal way has long been recognised. Requirements for the review of children in foster care were established in 1946 in the wake of the death of a child, Dennis Nolan, at the hands of his foster carers. Reviewing rules were set out in various versions of Boarding Out Regulations since that time and were reflected in legislation. However, developments leading to the introduction of the IRO did not really get going until the Children Act 1989, which heralded landmark reforms for children and is still the most important piece of legislation in relation to children in care. It has been generally amended by subsequent legislation, but remains the main point of reference, and this is certainly the case for IRO legislation.

Prior to 1989, there had been substantial concern about drift and delay in planning for children in care and this lay behind the Children Act requirements. Drift and delay is where decisions about the child's future are delayed for reasons of bureaucracy and inefficiency. It is in the child's best interests that long-term decisions are made as swiftly as appropriate. Regulations and guidance established by the Children Act placed more emphasis on the regular review of plans, and required that children and parents should participate in the reviewing process. However, at this point there was no suggestion that there should be an independent person with an independent perspective involved in the process.

Following the Children Act, a number of local authorities thought it would be helpful to bring some independence to the process and appointed officers who were separate from the line management of the cases concerned to conduct the reviews. There was, of course, no statutory requirement for this initiative, but it lay some groundwork for subsequent developments.

The Adoption and Children Act 2002

The Adoption and Children Act 2002 introduced the statutory requirement for 'independence' in the reviewing process, and effectively created the role of the IRO. The Act required 'all local authorities to have IROs in place to chair the statutory review meetings of all looked after children'. There was no suggestion that the IRO should be employed or managed by anyone other than the local authority.

A significant driver in this development was concern expressed by the courts in a number of cases that children made subject to care orders by a court, with quite specific care plans, had no recourse or route back to the court if the local authority failed to implement those plans or changed them significantly without justification. The 2002 Act gave the IRO the power to refer cases back to court through the Children and Family Court Advisory and Support Service (Cafcass), if the IRO believed that the local authority was seriously failing in its duty to the child. This option was available as a 'last resort' that could only be used when all other remedies had failed.

The requirements of the 2002 Act came into force for IROs in September 2004. However, doubts were soon being expressed about the effectiveness of the new arrangements and in particular the question of the genuine independence of IROs and their capacity to hold local authorities to account. In particular, could IROs be genuinely independent to challenge the local authority, and hold it to account, when they were employed by that local authority?

The Children and Young Persons Act 2008

The Children and Young Persons Act 2008 introduced measures that strengthened the role of the IRO but did not establish its independence from the local authority. This Act required that each child had a named IRO. It enabled the IRO to refer to Cafcass in a more straightforward way and not merely as a 'last resort'. The Act also established a 'sunset clause' that gave power to the Secretary of State within seven years from the passing of the Act to establish a separate management body for IROs if he or she decided that current arrangements were not working well. The sun went down in November 2015 without such other arrangements being made and the change is no longer available. There are many IROs who regret that more serious consideration to separate arrangements was not given.

The main components of the IRO role

While there are several important legal documents that underpin the IRO's role, the most important source, from the point of view of this chapter, is the *IRO Handbook*. This is statutory guidance, and it must be complied with unless there are powerful reasons not to do so. It is sometimes called the IRO's 'Bible'. It sets out all the main powers and duties of the IRO role, and I believe that all carers should be provided with a copy of this document and should understand its main provisions.

The powers and duties of the IRO set out in the *IRO Handbook* include:

- chairing the child's review

- critically scrutinising and monitoring the child's care plan from an independent point of view

- monitoring the performance of the local authority in relation to the child's case

- ensuring and promoting a child-centred reviewing process

- ensuring that the voice of the child is at the forefront of all processes

- promoting permanence – there should be a permanence plan in place from the second review.

In relation to the review meeting, the following should apply:

- It's the child's meeting. The child should influence when and where it is held, who attends and the agenda.

- The IRO must speak to the child privately prior to the review.

- The IRO must strongly involve the child (according to their age, understanding and capacity) and sometimes may hand over the chairing role to the child.

- The agenda should be tailored for the child's wishes and begin from the child's perspective.

There are various issues that must be considered in the review process and these are set out in the *IRO Handbook*. Among these are:

- changes since the last review
- implementation of decisions of the last review
- legal status
- permanence plan
- contact with family and other important people
- placement
- education
- health
- leisure activities.

This is not an exhaustive list.

Do IROs make recommendations or decisions? There had been much debate about whether the review makes recommendations (which the local authority can take or leave) or decisions (which are binding on the local authority). The *IRO Handbook* is clear that they are decisions. If the local authority disagrees with a decision, it must say so within five days, when a dispute resolution process would commence. The local authority must establish a formal dispute resolution process to use if there is disagreement.

Involvement of foster carers in the review process is crucial, and the *IRO Handbook* makes specific reference to this. It is expected that foster carers will be important members of the team around the child. The IRO and the foster carer should communicate with each other as often and as frequently as they see fit. More will be said about IROs and foster carers working together later in this chapter.

Employment arrangements for IROs

A survey by the National Children's Bureau (NCB) in 2013[1] found that:

- 94% of local authorities kept the IRO service in-house and located it within the children's services department

- 6% of authorities outsourced their IRO service

- 13% of IROs were self-employed or agency IROs.

The *IRO Handbook* recommends that IRO caseloads should be between 50 and 70 children in care. The NCB survey showed an average caseload for a full-time equivalent IRO was 78. However, on top of this, IROs were often given other jobs and duties within the local authority (most commonly chairing child protection conferences), which may have impaired their capacity to perform the IRO role effectively. Most IROs believe their capacity to do their job effectively is impaired by excessive workloads.

---

1   *The Role of Independent Reviewing Officers in England* (August 2013), National Children's Bureau.

IROs can sometimes find themselves in an isolated and vulnerable position, particularly when trying to undertake serious challenges of local authorities. External support is sometimes essential, particularly when management and support arrangements within the local authority are not as strong as they might be.

The National Association of Independent Reviewing Officers (NAIRO) was set up in 2010 as the professional body for IROs. It seeks to provide support for IROs, raise practice standards, provide training and influence policy. It is an important source of support for IROs who may be in need of it. NAIRO has also published a 'toolkit' for IROs that is an aid to promoting good practice.

The independence of IROs is one of the most contentious issues within the IRO community and for those who work with IROs. The question of whether IROs can effectively perform the role of challenger of the local authority, holding the local authority to account for plans which may not be in the interest of children, when they are directly employed by the local authority, is a live one.

Some IROs believe that they may be most effective within the local authority because they understand how the local authorities work and how the levers of influence may best be used. Others believe that being employed by the local authority compromises their independence and fetters their capacity to challenge effectively. There are stories of IROs being pressured or leaned on to water down their challenges.

In a 2014 survey conducted by NAIRO, the majority of members who responded thought IRO services were best placed within local authorities. However, 91% of respondents thought that there needed to be measures put in place to strengthen the IRO role and its independence and effectiveness if local authorities continued to manage IRO services.

The effectiveness of IROs

Since the introduction of the strengthened role of IROs in 2010 there have been three main studies about their effectiveness:

- The NCB study *The Role of Independent Reviewing Officers in England*, August 2013.

- The Ofsted report *Independent Reviewing Officers: Taking up the Challenge*, June 2013.

- The University of East Anglia report *Care Planning and the Role of the Independent Reviewing Officer*, October 2015.

A report entitled *Placement Disruption* on behalf of the Nationwide Association of Fostering Providers (NAFP) is also relevant. This report looked at the disruption of (on the face of it) good placements for children, for financial reasons. Disappointingly, IROs were not active in these cases in seeking to preserve the placement, and this may indicate that the IRO system is not always working as it should.

It is beyond the scope of this brief chapter to do more than give a very brief outline of conclusions reached by the research about the effectiveness of IROs. However, the following general points can be safely made:

- Practice is extremely variable. In some local authorities it would appear that the IRO service is working well and offering an effective protection for children in care. In other authorities it is not. A key challenge is to bring the practice of the worst-performing local authorities up to the best.

- Workloads are generally much too high, and the effectiveness of IRO performance is compromised by workloads that are considerably in excess of the recommended levels. Many IROs believe that the effectiveness of their work is compromised by their lack of real independence from local authority children's services management. The culture of children's services departments (and the extent to which they value or not the potential contribution of the IRO service) is a critical factor in their effectiveness. The quality of management arrangements available to support IROs in the difficult work they do is also a critical factor.

Foster carers and IROs working together

In order for the IRO to conduct their duties effectively it is essential that they work in close partnership with all the members of the team around the child. This includes the social worker, the supervising social worker from the fostering agency, education and health authorities, and most importantly (from the point of view of this chapter) the foster carers.

The Foster Carers' Charter was launched in 2011. The intention was to ensure that foster carers are given the respect, authority and support they need to enable them to do their job effectively. Although the charter does not have the status of statutory guidance, it was the government's hope that local authorities would sign up to it. It said that local authorities and fostering services must:

- recognise in practice the importance of the child's relationships with their foster family as one that can make the biggest difference in the child's life and that can endure into adulthood

- listen to and involve foster carers and their foster children in decision making and planning

- be sensitive to the needs of the foster carer and the child in making and ending placements

- treat foster carers with openness, fairness and respect as core members of the team around the child.

I believe IROs should do all they can to support the letter and the spirit of the charter, and this clearly involves working closely with foster carers in an open and respectful way. (For more about the Foster Carers' Charter see the Appendix at the end of this book.)

Monitoring the progress of the child and communication between IROs and carers

A key element of the role of the IRO is to monitor the progress of the child in placement. The most obvious and effective way to undertake this (when the child is in foster care) is to have close communication with the foster carer. After all, the foster carers are the people who know the child best and who can report most accurately and in an up-to-date manner on their progress. They are the child 'expert'. It is my view that a key element in the capacity of the IRO to conduct their role effectively is to enjoy full, frequent and unfettered communication with the foster carer. The IRO should ensure that the foster carer should have contact details for the IRO and should be able to be in touch with them whenever they wish to be. Similarly, the IRO should be able to contact the foster carer.

There may be occasions when this unfettered communication feels uncomfortable or is discouraged by the local authority. This is particularly likely to be the case when there are differences of opinion between the local authority and the foster carers, and the local authority may wish to implement a plan (for example, a termination of placement) with which the foster carers disagree. Open communication between the IRO and the carers is all the more important in these cases. I don't believe it is ever right for a local authority or other agency to seek to fetter the communication between IROs and foster carers. In the cases mentioned in the *Placement Disruption* report from NAFP it is evident that there was a failure of the IROs to work effectively with the foster carers.

Of course, it is not the case that the IRO will always agree with the foster carers against the local authority on what is in the interests of the child. Doubtless on many occasions the IRO will disagree with the foster carer. It simply means that IROs must have full access to all the views and information of all the parties involved in the care of the child and must in particular consult carefully with the foster carers.

The importance of relationships in promoting recovery for children in care

The Care Inquiry Report *Making not Breaking* of April 2013 found that positive relationships were the most important thing for children in care. Positive relationships must be nurtured, supported and protected.

A crucial part of the IRO's role is to promote, nurture and protect beneficial relationships for children in care. The most important of these relationships is likely to be with foster carers – hence the need for close working relationships between the IRO and foster carers.

It is well known that the most common reason for children and young people coming into care is serious abuse or neglect. The latest figure for this is 60%,[2] although this probably rather understates the true position.

What is most important in promoting healing and recovery from abuse is the provision of safe, affectionate, long-term relationships with trustworthy adults. These relationships must be characterised by a high degree of empathy, warmth and long-term commitment. Adults providing these relationships must be carefully selected and have access to high-quality specialist training and support. IROs have a role in supporting foster carers in providing these crucial relationships for children.

---

2   Looked-after Children Statistics 2016, Department for Education.

It will sometimes be the case that fostering panels need to take decisions about foster carers (perhaps in relation to limiting, changing or ending their registration) which will have an impact on children currently being cared for by those foster carers. In such cases, it is important that the IRO is able to have a good line of communication with the panel and the panel chair in order to inform them of their concerns and views.

IROs have a crucial role in promoting the welfare of children in care and ensuring that local authority plans are in their best interests and promote good practice. IROs must at all times listen carefully to the voice of the child and make sure that the child's views are properly understood and taken into full account in any decision-making procedure.

It is essential that close working relationships are established between IROs and foster carers and that there is full and unfettered communication between them. This is particularly important where there may be disagreement or conflict between different members of the team around the child.

Conclusion

Always remember that whether or not you regard yourself as a professional you are the expert on the child that you are looking after. This means you should not feel cowed or unimportant when working with the professionals in the team around the child. If you feel that you are being marginalised or that your views are not being taken into account, then talk to your social worker and never be afraid to advocate for your child.

Chapter 11

SPECIAL GUARDIANSHIP ORDERS

—— Andy Elvin and John Simmonds OBE ——

A relatively new order known as a special guardianship order (SGO) was introduced in legislation in 2002 and in practice in 2005. An SGO is most like an adoption order in that if you take an SGO in respect of your foster child you will become the legal parents of the child. However, the legal parental responsibility of the birth parents is not extinguished. As the holder of the SGO you will still be able to make all decisions and choices for your child without conferring with or seeking the permission of the birth parents, but the order does not extinguish the birth parents' legal parental responsibility in the way that an adoption order does. Though legally there is not a huge difference between an adoption order and an SGO, emotionally and psychologically there is an enormous difference. Knowing that their status as the legal birth parents remains and that no new birth certificate will be issued so that the birth certificate the child takes through life will continue to have their name on it is hugely significant both emotionally and psychologically to birth parents, and so applications for SGOs are often significantly less fraught than for adoption orders.

The two groups most likely to apply for SGOs are the child's foster carers and members of the child's extended family. We concentrate here on foster carers who seek to take SGOs but also touch on the fact that some foster carers work with family members who take on the care of the children and move to apply for SGOs. This can happen when relatives emerge as potential carers during care proceedings, and children who may have been with foster carers in the short term will have the option of being placed with an extended family member at the end of the proceedings.

The introduction of special guardianship in the amendments made to the Children Act 1989 by the Adoption and Children Act 2002 has been significant. The original policy argument in the design of special guardianship was that there needed to be an order to enable a child's foster carers to exercise parental responsibility to the exclusion of all others but without terminating the child's legal relationship with their birth parents or birth family. It was argued that there were groups of children who would benefit from the availability of such an order – those from minority ethnic and religious groups who could not or did not accept adoption, unaccompanied asylum-seeking children, older children whose relationship with their birth parents continued to be important, and children placed with family members or with long-term foster carers. The Adoption White Paper 2000[1] set out the proposal for such an order, and as this was developed, the new arrangements for the provision of adoption support services, including the statutory right to an assessment, were included in the design of special guardianship. As such the two orders (adoption and SGO) had very similar support arrangements, with the government making it clear that the permanency plan for the child should not be determined by the availability of the support package. In other words there being more support available for adopters should not lead to adoption being prioritised by Judges over an SGO with a relative.

---

1   www.gov.uk/government/uploads/system/uploads/attachment_data/ file/263529/5017.pdf

The implementation of the Adoption and Children Act 2002 at the end of 2005 saw the successful introduction of special guardianship.[2] Since its implementation there has been a steady rise in the number of children leaving care through special guardianship. Research by Hall (2008) identified that a significant number of these were made to extended family members. These findings were reinforced by Wade (2010), who noted 86% of orders being made to family and friends in the first two years following the implementation of SGOs. This high rate of orders made to family and friends has continued and was reinforced in a further study by Wade *et al.* (2014).

Primary and secondary legislation makes special guardianship a particularly flexible legal order with a range of people eligible to apply[3] (Simmonds 2011) – those in 'time established relationships' (e.g. children who have lived with relatives for some time or who have a significant relationship) and those where consent has been given or it is agreed that the order is in the child's best interests. An SGO is a private law order so cannot be made in favour of the local authority only named individuals. The local authority are generally ordered to make the assessment of the prospective Special Guardians. This includes addressing those issues that the special guardian will need in the provision of support. That flexibility is reinforced by the legislation saying that 'a court may make a special guardianship order with respect to a child in family proceedings…when the court considers that a special guardianship order should be made even though no such application has been made. In other words, the Judge can make an SGO to a relative even if the local authority, or other party, have not asked them to.

---

2   Section 14A, Special Guardianship Orders, Adoption and Children Act 2002.
3   Section 14A(5).

Psychological parenting

The development of placement practice over the last 50 years has paid particular attention to the child's subjective experience of parenting. From a young child's point of view it is the person who directly cares for them who is the parent, whatever the legal definition or the adult's perspective. We have moved away from the belief that parents have rights over their child to seeing parents having responsibilities to their child. This has evolved into the concept of the 'psychological parent' – the person who 'does' the parenting.

A baby has little, if any, control over who their parent is experienced as being. They will respond to the person who presents themselves as the parent and will quickly build expectations that this person is their carer through the intimacy of the interactions that take place on a minute-by-minute basis and then over time. For the baby there is an inherent expectation arising out of and embedded in the primary requirement that the child is kept safe and their needs are met by a competent adult who can survive the challenges of what for a small child is a high-risk environment. Young children in temporary foster care may see their foster carer as a stranger and experience the separation from their parent as a significant loss. However, they adjust to their new carer relatively quickly and this may be particularly so where previous experience has been marked by neglect or abuse. The temporary foster carer is experienced as the child's psychological parent, whatever the foster carer, social worker or birth parents' perspective on this might be. The child may have to make some – possibly significant – adjustments, but it is their subjective experience that needs to be understood and taken into account. The same issues are probably true for older children as well, but this is also likely to be made complex when children have significant experience of others as parental figures – their birth parents in particular – and have formed a strong bond even if this is marked by abuse and neglect. They may be drawn to their new carers as safer, more sensitive and responsive people, but the embedded memories of high-risk adults from their past are likely to live on.

Children make significant adjustments in their own minds about who their parents are based on day-to-day experience, but these adjustments typically involve uncertainty, anxiety and loss. The child's drive to seek and experience security, familiarity and commitment from their primary carers cannot be underestimated. At the same time, the challenge for the child and the adult carers in doing so cannot be underestimated, especially when this has been marked by ongoing experiences of abuse and neglect and the serious unpredictability that typically accompanies this.

It has become central to the preparation of foster carers and adopters that these children-focused matters are understood. The impact on carers in responding to the child's adjustment in the short and longer term can be significant, especially where there are high levels of anxiety, fear or loss for the child. There is evidence that some carers see the child's anxiety and reluctance to respond to their new carers as the child just 'being undemanding', while others may see this as 'difficult' or 'naughty'. The development of new relationships and patterns of relating is complex and requires insight, support and time.

There are also important issues connected to the carer's motivation to foster or adopt – their own experiences of being parented, their current views and experiences of being a parent, and the support that is available to them both within and outside their family. Flexibility, adapting to the 'new' and unexpected situations and then learning from experience will play an important part in this. This will always include the need for access to practical, housing and financial support. Most people have questions that need to be explored, and this has become a key part of the preparation and assessment for fostering, and the answers to these questions core to being approved as suitable foster carers.

Taking an SGO as a foster carer

If you have had a child placed with you for 18 months to two years and the plan is that the child remains with you throughout their childhood, then the local authority responsible for the child may raise the subject of an SGO with you.

One advantage of taking an SGO is that a lot of the statutory furniture will be removed from your life. The record-keeping, professional meetings, reviews and visits by social workers and other professionals will cease. This may be very important to the child and can also be welcome to some foster carers. The removal of the statutory framework does not mean that you should isolate yourself from professional support. It is advisable to get an agreement from the local authority or your fostering agency that you can still call them for support and advice, that you can still attend training for foster carers or adopters and that you will still have their support in accessing, for example, child and adolescent mental health services or other therapeutic interventions should they be required to help you care for your child. SGOs are not a magical panacea for issues that your child might face during their development.

It is advisable to have the conversations with the local authority and with your fostering agency before broaching the subject of an SGO with the young person. It is also recommended that you discuss the decision in depth with your social worker, as taking an SGO is a significant step and is worth appropriate reflection and discussion so that you are fully aware of the implications and you are confident in the support that you will be offered, before you talk to the young person. It would, of course, be hugely detrimental to the young person and possibly to the placement if you discussed the issue with them first and then discovered that the local authority was not prepared to offer the financial and ongoing professional support that you felt you needed to successfully bring up the child.

What foster carers who have taken SGOs have told us

TACT undertook some research in 2014/15 with foster carers who had taken SGOs.

Once an SGO is granted, the child is no longer in the care system, and therefore the child and their carers do not qualify for any of the support and advice available to other children in care. A key milestone in any young person's life is the transition to adulthood. Young people who are under special guardianship arrangements are denied access to any post-18 support. Many of the children and young people under SGOs have been in the care system or on the edge of care and have suffered abuse and neglect before they entered the care system. It is therefore vital they have access to the same support services as those in the care system and those leaving care at 18 years. The foster carers in the survey were clear that support packages for special guardians and children were an essential element of the SGO process. In addition to support packages being in line with other permanency options, there also needs to be a mechanism to regularly review the package, because support needs are not static.

Forty per cent of the foster carers felt that the legislative framework needed to be more closely aligned to other permanence options such as adoption or long-term foster care. One foster carer commented that social services should be available to the children under SGOs until they turn 18 years: 'I needed the social services but it got cut out after a year.'

The foster carers were very clear that SGOs were successful and beneficial to children when the order was used in the right circumstances and the right support was provided to the special guardians and the child. It is a concern that SGOs appear to be being used in cases where it is not appropriate as a cheap alternative to long-term foster care, and in some cases pressure is being applied to foster carers to apply for orders, otherwise the child will be moved on. Some of the foster carers had experienced local authorities applying this pressure at different stages in the placement.

At the referral stage

Agencies are seeing a trend in local authority referral information about children who have just entered the care system asking for foster carers who would move to or consider special guardianship arrangements. For example, at TACT we received a referral for a child of nine years of age who had been living with short-term foster carers for two years. The local authority referral information stated that they were looking to place the child with foster carers who were able to care for the child on a permanent basis and would be willing to move to an SGO. This appears to be against the original policy intention of SGOs, which states that an application for an SGO may be made by a foster carer once the child has lived with them for at least a year. The current statutory guidance does not provide for introductory, matching or settling-in periods, as with adoption, and therefore the expectation is that there will be a pre-existing relationship between the child and special guardian.

At the start of the placement

Agencies are increasingly seeing local authorities making placements on the condition that special guardianship is part of the care plan or that SGOs are considered soon after the placement has started. TACT has many referrals of this nature from local authorities across the country. Carers are very uncomfortable with this.

During the placement

Social workers and foster carers have reported a number of examples in recent years of local authorities continuously applying pressure on them to move to special guardianship, as is demonstrated in the case study below.

CASE STUDY

The foster carer has been caring for the ten-year-old boy for two years and is currently considering applying for an SGO for fear of losing the child, as the local authority wants to pursue special guardianship. The child is extremely settled in his current placement. The local authority has considered a family member as a potential special guardian but they were not suitable to care for the child. The IRO, school and advocate are all in favour of long-term foster care and are opposed to pursuing the option of an SGO for fear of lack of support post-order. The foster carer has now said that she will consider an SGO to ensure stability for the child. She feels that as soon as she notified social services that she would consider an SGO 'everything changed and it became a rushed process'. The local authority has stated that it will match the carers' allowance but none of this has been put in writing as yet. Throughout this process the child has always said that he does not want to move and frequently talks about his future with the foster carers.

Recent research showed that more than two-fifths of carers felt some sort of pressure from the local authority to move on to an SGO, with one in five special guardians feeling strong pressure by local authorities to accept an SGO (Wade *et al.* 2014). A key factor in this is the squeezed timescales to meet the 26-week care proceedings limit, which are constraining the time to adequately prepare special guardians for the challenges ahead. This pressure, combined with the lack of settling-in time, is a cause of great concern.

In the survey there were mixed experiences of the foster carers in how SGOs were raised as an option and pressure applied to proceed with an order as a permanence option. A number of the carers had not heard of an SGO before, but the local authority provided all the information and advice they needed to make an informed decision, while others felt pressurised to take out an SGO, otherwise the child would be moved. They were informed by the local authority that this was a cost-saving exercise.

> 'It was suggested by the local authority as a cost-saving exercise... I was under the impression that if we did not move to an SGO the child would be moved on. There was an element of force involved... Adoption was considered but the birth mother was strongly against it.'

Two foster carers felt pressure from social services to take out an order because the children in their care were being considered for adoption and there was the possibility of sibling groups being split up because only the younger sibling was likely to be adopted. The carers wanted the children to be kept together and felt that the SGO was the best option for the children.

One foster carer commented on the pressure from the local authority:

> 'If I didn't take the SGO, the children would have been removed. That's a lot of pressure, since they have been living with me for two years.'

One carer was approached by the local authority to consider an SGO, even though the birth parents would not work with the local authority or the carer:

> 'I felt that the local authority wanted me to be left to deal with an impossible contact situation by myself. I felt it was an easy way out for the local authority.'

Of the nine foster carers interviewed who have gone through the SGO assessment process, four felt that the process did not need to be improved and four felt that it did. One carer could not remember the assessment process because she went through it a number of years ago. The length of time taken for the assessment varied greatly from two weeks to one year.

'From my point of view it was rushed through. Two assessments were done within 48 hours in order to put it in front of a judge.'

'My husband and I thought the assessment was very thorough. The child is not the same race as us so the assessing social worker wanted to ensure that everything was covered in terms of race and culture. The assessment was very in depth and covered absolutely everything. I felt this was very reassuring as they had the best interests of the child in mind throughout.'

Some carers received access to a solicitor during the assessment process. All those who received impartial legal advice felt it was useful in developing the contact arrangements and the support package.

A number of those interviewed felt that if you are already an approved foster carer you should not have to go through the full assessment process for special guardians. The information from Form F could be used and a fast-track process adopted. However, some foster carers felt that the assessment was not thorough enough and the assessing social worker did not go into any depth because it was assumed they would be suitable if they were foster carers.

Negotiating the contact arrangements was a key issue during the assessment process for some carers. One foster carer said that the contact agreement restricted visits from the birth mother to three times a year, and when she requested the option for the mother to have increased visits she was told she could arrange what she wanted after the order. Another carer said that the children did not want to have contact with their birth father but the contact agreement gave him two visits per year.

One foster carer felt the assessment was 'unpleasant and intrusive'. The assessing social worker counted all the drawers in her house and commented that she would receive no help after the order. The carer commented that although the foster care assessment was far more in depth than the special guardian assessment she was always made to feel comfortable during the foster care assessment, whereas throughout the SGO assessment she felt exposed and intruded on.

None of the foster carers interviewed received preparation training as part of the assessment process, and yet all foster carers felt this would have been useful because many had not heard of special guardianship orders before they started the process.

Foster carers who are applying for SGOs and are approved carers with a pre-existing relationship with a child of at least one year should have the information from their Form F integrated into the SGO assessment process to avoid duplication. According to one foster carer who cares for a child under SGO arrangements:

> 'Because of the child's background and subsequent needs due to the trauma experienced, you never know what is going to come up in the future, and what worries me is that you are just left to handle things by yourself.'

Some special guardians and children under SGOs do not want any support post-order. The SGO can mark a new start and an end to working with social services, and a normalising of the relationship between the special guardian and the child:

> 'It benefited us to not have someone [social worker] coming back and forth, and it made her feel like it's a normal relationship.'

> 'The household is more of a regular family life without social workers.'

> 'The SGO is fine. The best part of it is not dealing with social workers.' (14-year-old under an SGO)

Many foster carers interviewed felt strongly that there should be a point of contact within social services who had responsibility for the families and children post-order. Some carers received support from social services for the first year of the order but the majority did not. A couple of foster carers commented that they still called on their agency social worker for support and advice because they had foster care placements with the agency as well as children under special guardianship arrangements.

> 'It would be nice to have a name and number available that you can call when things get difficult.'

> 'I feel alone. I don't know who to go to for help.'

One carer recently contacted the local authority for advice as she had experienced a problem with her child who had entered adolescence. She reported that the local authority support worker was 'reluctant to help'.

> 'The special guardianship experience has been strange because as a foster carer [you are] used to having a social worker to talk to about any issues that arise. Special guardians have not got this, and given the extent of the child's needs we feel like we've just been left to deal with it all... Given [the child's] needs it's the same as fostering but without the support.'

Support
Financial support
The financial support received by the special guardians interviewed was means tested on an annual basis. Some carers were receiving financial support from the local authority until their child left full-time education, whereas others had financial support for the first few years post-order. Other carers had had to fight the local authority to continue to receive financial support:

'
'The local authority tried to stop [financial support] after two years and I fought that decision. Then they tried to cut the money in half, but I fought that decision too.'

Peer support
A couple of the foster carers interviewed felt a peer support group for special guardians would be really useful so they were not 'set adrift and alone'.

Support for children under SGO arrangements
There needs to be more support for the educational and emotional needs of children under SGOs. Special guardians were determined that the child would get the same access to therapeutic support as their siblings living in foster care placements.

'[The child] should not be penalised because she was under an SGO and not in foster care.'

'There is a lack of support and children are usually forgotten about after the SGO. My big issue is the education side of it. There is not enough support for my children...'

Many of the foster carers felt that the children in their care needed support from social services until they turned 18 years.

The following comments were made by the special guardians who were interviewed in terms of what constitutes good practice to make the SGO a success.

'It is important for special guardians to have information about financial support. It is hard to take care of a child without financial support.'

'You need constant support. I feel like once the special guardian order is passed everyone washes their hands. I went into it naively because she didn't present with so

many problems to begin with. I think if we had known the extent of the problems we would have insisted on more support.'

'...a good relationship with the children and listening to what they want. Their views are very important, and it is a big commitment for both the child and the special guardian.'

'...having a solid knowledge of what the children are like and clear communication with the local authority.'

'I wouldn't recommend special guardianship to anyone because if you don't know the [birth] parents I wouldn't entertain it. I think it's a scary road to go down because you are left on your own, and if you are doing contact you're the one who has to call time. Lots of headaches, contact is the main one but also support; children should get the same package under different types of placement – they have the same needs.'

A major issue in deciding to take an SGO is managing contact arrangements with the birth parents. Contact with birth parents and the birth family can be very important to the child.

Some of the special guardians interviewed said it was difficult to manage complex contact situations with birth families, some of whom had special needs and chaotic lifestyles. One special guardian said it was stressful being responsible for 'calling time' on contact and dealing with the aftermath if the birth parents did not turn up to contact or if it was a stressful contact session. A number of special guardians commented that the contact arrangements were not the same as those agreed in court, and some said they felt this was an area that was 'neglected' in the process.

Social workers have reported special guardians going back to social services following the order for assistance in supervising contact or mediation with the birth parents.

CASE STUDY

We were surprised, 14 years ago, as brand new foster carers, to be asked to consider an SGO. Our then foster child had been with us only a matter of weeks. We were still getting to know each other and we had never heard of this latest acronym in the fostering alphabet. Neither did we yet know many other foster carers. Those who had been granted an SGO warned us to avoid it, and regarded it as a cost-cutting, responsibility-avoiding, future-proofing exercise for the sole benefit of the local authority. Sadly, a few felt they had been 'bounced' into an SGO.

Ten years on, with a new fostering agency and with much more experience, we were drawn to the possibility of seeking an SGO. Circumstances were right, we felt, for the following reasons:

- We all saw an SGO as a commitment just as significant as adoption, and felt it would cement our relationship with our youngster in a formal and legal way.

- Our youngster wanted to be free of the 'system' – social workers, meetings, slow and remote decisions, forms – but most of all, she did not want to be called 'fostered' or 'in care' any longer.

- After five years with the child we felt we had grown good attachments.

- We were aware of the difficulties that can arise in teenage years, and felt equipped to source the professional help we might need.

There was much for our youngster to consider, who was asked only after the basis of the SGO had been agreed. Any failure of negotiations or even abandonment of the process would have led to huge disappointment and almost certainly a severe loss of trust.

- Was she happy that we would be her legal parents, making decisions?

- Would she miss having access to a social worker (and someone to blame)?

- How would contact with her birth family be going forward now that we would organise and supervise that?

- What might she hope to do at 16 and 18 years, and beyond?

Once asked, she was delighted and readily agreed. Even after that it was a needlessly lengthy, wasteful and expensive process, though ultimately successful. Unusually, she came to court for the granting of the order and was impressed that the kindly circuit judge had clearly taken the trouble to read all about her. Later, she wrote to the Minister for Children about her experience and was delighted to receive a thoughtful and encouraging personal reply.

CASE STUDY

It is sometimes said that the one time to be selfish about marriage is before making the vows. Much the same could be said of the commitment involved in seeking an SGO for a child in care, in the sense that all key matters should be agreed before the SGO is agreed, since they are unlikely to be changed subsequently.

SGOs for children and young people currently being fostered are only likely to be suitable in a minority of cases, for a variety of reasons. But it can represent a marvellous alternative to long-term foster care into adulthood with existing foster carer(s) where:

- there is little realistic prospect of the child or young person returning home

- the placement is stable and the child or young person has a good attachment to the foster carer(s)

- the child or young person wants to be out of the 'care' system, to be as much like their friends as possible and to be regarded (if not already) as part of the family

- the child has a continuing wish to see one or both birth parents

- the foster carer(s) are willing and able to make the necessary commitment up to and possibly beyond 18; to source help when needed and accept a greater measure of responsibility

- the future needs of the child or young person – for example, in terms of health, education and therapeutic support – can be predicted with reasonable certainty

- there is a good relationship between the foster carer(s) and birth parent(s) and that the latter support the process (if that is important to the child or young person)

- there is a good relationship between the foster carer(s), the fostering agency and the relevant local authority; in particular that foster carer(s) do not feel pressured into seeking an SGO.

It's a difficult decision. By their nature, foster carers are committed to helping the youngsters in their care. It is all too easy to find themselves in a tricky position where the child or young person has been led to expect an SGO – even when no promise has been made – and then (for example) the local authority unexpectedly seeks to impose unacceptable conditions.

Whether or not the initiative for an SGO comes from the foster carer or from the local authority, foster carers would always be well advised to instruct a well-regarded solicitor with experience in family law in general and SGOs in particular. That solicitor can then write formally to the local authority setting out the foster carer's intention to apply for an SGO and broadly the terms on which they would be prepared to take the child or young person out of care. This takes much of the emotion out of the situation and also signals to the local authority that the foster carers won't just roll over and accept whatever the local authority might offer financially and in terms of ongoing professional support. Professional legal involvement gives the best prospect of a robust SGO agreement that all parties are content with.

Once that broad agreement is reached, it is the time to seek the permission of all concerned to broach the subject with the child or young person...and start planning for the eventual celebration.

Conclusion

Many foster carers have now taken SGOs and the feedback is largely positive, with most being pleased that they have taken this step. It is worth noting that many do talk of some of the battles they have had in accessing continuing professional support, which is why it is so important that you have a tangible written agreement about this before taking an SGO. Particularly important in this is the issue of contact, so it is vital that you feel that contact arrangements are agreed and that any support you feel you may need is agreed before you apply for the order.

Chapter 12

WELL-BEING

—— Andy Elvin ——

Foster care can be tough, as any parenting can be. Alongside the challenges the day-to-day care of a foster child may bring, there will also be the challenges of dealing with the wider professional network and some of the statutory obligations that come with the care system. For this reason it is important that you look after yourself as a foster carer. Sometimes it is helpful to think of your emotional spirit level. Events, behaviours, expectations and challenges may throw your spirit level off and it's important to recognise when this is happening. You should always reflect on this with your supervising social worker, and they should also check out how you are, how you are feeling and how you are coping in your role as a foster carer.

There are many avenues for self-care. One of the most important is your support network and staying in touch with them, often for advice, support or just to vent about things that have happened. Your agency should run carer support groups, so try to get along to these as often as you can; even if you think things are going well, it never hurts to sit and to swap stories and discuss things that are going on with your respective foster children. Other foster carers are an invaluable resource; reach out to them when you want advice. In turn, it is important to be available to others to offer them support; your perspective, your experiences and your expertise may be absolutely vital to the foster carer who is going through a rough time. Giving such support is often also hugely beneficial for your own well-being.

As for any parent, it's important that you also make time for yourself, so do try to continue to follow outside interests and to make time to do the things that relax and rejuvenate you. Though this can be a challenge given the demands that foster care will sometimes place on you, it is important to prioritise your well-being when possible.

The most important thing is not to stay silent when you're struggling. You will not be alone as a foster carer – your agency and your supervising social worker are there to support you, and so you should reach out to them and to other foster carers when you feel you need that support.

Below are two case studies from foster carers detailing how they look out for their well-being.

CASE STUDY

Rob and I always look out for each other. If a child is having an emotional outburst, it can be very challenging and frustrating. I know I'm prone sometimes to getting a bit 'teeth gritted' in those situations. Rob will always say 'Go and have a cup of tea' and take over. We have an agreement to *always* take that advice from each other; I've known folk in the past who feel they have to finish what they've started, but sometimes letting someone else take over is the right thing to do, and gives the child a new scenario in which they can behave differently.

A cup of tea and scribbling bullet points on a piece of paper for the diary later on can get my perspective back, and I can then go back, if the situation isn't resolved, and try to help the child move on. I do the same for Rob if his patience is wearing thin. We're none of us saints, and it's only human to get frustrated from time to time.

We both have our own hobbies and make sure that we have time to do them away from the house. Our grown-up son once said it was a bit like 'tag fostering' sometimes – one of us would be away for a day one weekend and the other the next! It's great to see our friends and talk about something totally different. You can get to the state when all of your conversations with each other are about the children – that's not healthy for us, or for the children either, as it must feel a bit like being under a microscope at times. It's good for them to know that people have several different social circles, as well as being good for us to relax and catch our breath.

Short breaks are so important. We rarely go away but it's lovely to just laze around the house for a change, go out together, recharge. We talk about the children in a more relaxed manner and look back on how they've matured and changed over their time with us. We also spend time looking forwards, making plans. When the children come back it's great to see them, knowing they've had a lovely time as well.

CASE STUDY

Both of us have taken advantage of early retirement packages and are financially secure. We are home owners who enjoy socialising, overseas travel and dining out. Unfortunately, we have no children of our own. However, with no ties, this has enabled us to be spontaneous in relation to our leisure time.

Having been introduced to the concept of fostering by close friends, we were of the belief we possessed the time, abilities and desire to provide a secure long-term family environment for a young person. Our lack of children had always been a regret, and accordingly it was our intention to move to a permanency situation as soon as possible.

Rose, who was seven and a half at the time, entered our home some two and a half years ago and, in general, matters have worked out exactly as we had hoped.

There is no birth parent involvement and a date for a permanency hearing has been confirmed. We hope that in a matter of weeks Rose's long-term future will be secured. Thereafter, adoption is a strong possibility.

Friends and family, although fully supportive from the outset, were somewhat concerned that we would very soon discover that having full responsibility for a young child could be restrictive and would impact greatly on our day-to-day lives. In short, we would be unable to enjoy the lifestyle to which we had become accustomed. This was an aspect of fostering which was also covered in detail during the excellent induction training provided by our local agency.

Taking heed of the advice provided, we determined at an early stage to manage the change to our circumstances in an effort to maximise our chances of success and to assist us in coping with the numerous stressful situations that would undoubtedly emerge. The strategy we decided on was built round certain key areas. In no particular order:

- To ensure that family and friends would be part of Rose's new life from the outset. Through regular visits, outings and family gatherings Rose is now regarded by all as part of our family and is treated no differently from any other family member or friend. Perhaps we were fortunate, but we did not encounter any resistance to our new circumstances.

- To each continue to do the activities we enjoyed and maintain regular contact with friends and family. Rose is included in these activities at times, but each of us also 'gets to do our own thing' from time to time. With a little bit of give and take, and to the surprise of most, we continue to enjoy the exact same things we always have. This is despite taking on full-time responsibility for a young person at a time when most retirees are looking for a quieter life.

- To establish an effectual support network and utilise the help and expertise on offer. In addition to family and friends, we have developed an excellent relationship with our agency support worker, our local school, the parents of Rose's classmates, doctor, dentist, optician and the local Cub Scout group leadership. Each area of our support network has assisted us through tough challenges, not only in a practical sense but also by offering advice, guidance, experience and reassurance when called on.

- To be honest with each other. At times it has been very tough, and it's fair to say that, particularly in the early days, each of us has had doubts about our ability or desire to continue along the fostering path. By being open and honest with each other, we managed to resolve any issues, usually involving a less stressful approach. Sometimes it's good to just talk.

- To attend training workshops. The agency hosts an excellent range of workshops covering all aspects of working with looked-after children; for example, attachment and brain development, tears and tantrums, dealing with loss, foetal alcohol syndrome. Attending these sessions has not only helped us in a practical sense but has also prepared us for situations which may or may not arise and also helped us to get things in perspective at times. Sharing experiences with fellow carers has also been of great benefit in identifying ways to resolve issues and helping to reduce that feeling of being 'all alone'. It somehow helps to know that others are experiencing the same trials and tribulations.

- To be positive and to continually remind ourselves of our reasons for fostering. We found it extremely rewarding to take time to reflect on the progress that had been achieved and to acknowledge Rose's development, both physically and mentally.

Bringing Rose into our lives has meant wholesale changes to our daily lives and at times has been exceptionally stressful. It is impossible to avoid that stress, but by adopting the strategy just outlined, we feel we have managed to cope fairly well. So much so, we are now enjoying the benefits of the family environment we always wanted to create. We still enjoy the things we always did and we still enjoy an active social life. The only difference is that Rose is now an integral part of those activities. Rose has been good for us as a couple and as people.

Conclusion

By looking after yourselves you look after your children. Always be sure to check your emotional spirit level on at least a weekly basis, and do not neglect hobbies and interests that bring you enjoyment. As a foster carer you are the primary resource, so it is important that you don't allow yourself to burn out. Taking time for yourself is not selfish or uncaring; it is vital, and it is in the best interests of the child in your care.

Chapter **13**

ENDINGS

—— Martin Barrow ——

Saying goodbye

When we talk to friends about our work as foster carers, the most common response is: 'We couldn't do it, because we could never say goodbye.'

Saying goodbye is, without a doubt, one of the most difficult aspects of foster care. How can it be otherwise? You receive a child into your home, sometimes for many months; help them to come to terms with some of the most challenging issues; shelter them from the worst the world can hurl at them; watch them grow physically and emotionally. You share moments that are precious and moments that are distressing. You laugh together and, occasionally, cry together, although you do your best to hide your tears.

Then, one day, it all comes to an end, as it must do. The car is packed, there is barely time for one last hug, and you wave goodbye. The front door closes, and the house falls quiet.

It gets no easier with experience. As I write this chapter, a permanency plan is taking shape to find permanent homes for the three siblings who have lived with us for 15 months. Our focus is on making the transition as easy as possible for our foster children. But we are under no illusions about how difficult this will also be for us.

We also are aware that their departure will affect other members of our family, including our daughters and grandson, and a far wider community, from teachers and classmates at school to the extended fostering team who have supported their care. All will be saying good-bye to children who have become such an integral part of their lives.

We are short-term foster carers, although what we do stretches the definition of the phrase 'short term'. When we agree to a placement we assume that it will last for at least a year. We generally care for siblings, and the range of ages is from newborn to early teens. For the youngest, the time they spend in care with us accounts for a substantial slice of their lives. When they leave, they may have little recollection of anything other than living with us.

With each and every placement we have gone through the agony of considering whether we should, and could, offer a permanent home to children who we have, undoubtedly, come to love. Yet each time we have decided against it.

There are a number of reasons, not least of which is now our age (we are in our mid-50s). But at the heart of our decision is a belief that what we do best is embrace children at a deep time of crisis, offer sanctuary, rebuild trust and confidence, and help them discover a world that is kind, generous and full of wonder. When they move on, our foster children will be making room for other boys and girls who need the same love and care.

We remind ourselves of this commitment, to assuage our doubts when the question of permanency comes around. It has become integral to the way that we, as a family, manage the difficult process of saying goodbye.

In a sense, preparation for the moment children will leave you begins almost from the moment they arrive. As their foster carer, one of your first duties will be to capture that moment as a memory to share with them when they are older. It will be recounted in your diary notes, and become the opening page in their memory book. One day they will open their memory book, and your words, and your kindness, will be with them.

Memories are an important part of foster care, and an important aspect of helping a child to move on. For most children and young people, their birth families are the primary source of memories. Mums and dads, grandparents, aunts and uncles, siblings, close family friends – all contribute to a vast pool of knowledge that informs memory and defines a child's identity. First steps, first words, first day at school, learning to ride a bike, starring in the Christmas play; these are defining moments that are normally witnessed by loved ones. They become part of family folklore, recorded for posterity through photos and anecdotes and, these days, shared with a wider circle of friends through social media.

When a child comes into care this pool of knowledge is broken, sometimes temporarily, sometimes forever. The way the care process works it is almost inevitable that a child will live with more than one foster carer. Each time a child says goodbye and moves on, there is a risk that memories that are essential to define identity, which will help them understand who they are, will be lost.

In this regard, a foster carer's responsibility is enormous. You become the keeper of memories. Whether a child moves back to the family, or on to foster care or adoption, they will look to you as the source of the life stories that they have missed. For example, they will want to know whether an infant has had measles, but they also will be interested to know the story of the infant's measles – what they were like in the build-up, how long it took to clear, what you gave the child to cheer them up. In effect, you have to fill in the details that all mums and dads want to be able to share when they talk to their friends and family. One day, they will be passed on to the child, who will then be able to share them with their own children. All this is possible because you made a note of how it was, and took the trouble to include it in the memory book (with the traditional photograph of the child with spots).

Luckily, digital photography and the high quality of cameras on mobile phones has made it so much easier (and inexpensive) to record moments. We have taken many more pictures of our foster children than of our own daughters, who grew up when digital photography was still in its infancy. We have plenty of choice when it comes to selecting the pictures for their memory books to illustrate the life stories. We also compile separate photo albums for each child, and give a memory disk with all the photographs on for their parents or carers.

It is never too soon to start collecting memories. Paintings, writing, notes from teachers, swimming certificates, medals from gym clubs, brochures from castles and farm parks – all have a significance that will help a child connect with their past. Of course, not everything can find its way into memory boxes, but it is better to save too much, than to not have enough. This is particularly important when you cannot be sure how long a placement will last. Collect memories that appear meaningful to you, as a carer and as a parent, but be mindful that this is for somebody else, a person probably unknown to you or the children, as yet.

Record a child's stay with you in as much detail as possible. Here are some of the things you should include:

- descriptions of what the child was like when they arrived; what they liked and disliked

- details of development (learning to swim, ride a bike, ice skate)

- special memories

- birthdays, Christmas and other family celebrations, outings and holidays, favourite places

- details and photos of your family (including extended family), home, pets

- school – photos, certificates, reports, photos of and stories from teachers

- contact visits

- significant illnesses

- funny stories and amusing quotes

- crafts, pictures and work completed in your home, at school and at playgroup.

Think about mementos that will help children remember special celebrations or outings. For example, we ask each child to choose a bauble to hang on the Christmas tree, which they can take with them when they move on. One of our children likes to play a particular card game, so we have already packed a set for her.

Preparing children to move on

When children arrive, you are unlikely to know how long the placement will last, or what the outcome will be. Even when a plan begins to take shape, there are likely to be twists and turns before a final decision is reached.

Amid such uncertainty, children are bound to ask questions about their futures. Your response will be informed by the particulars of each case. Some children will have their hopes set on returning home to mum and dad, while others fear being sent back to homes where they have suffered harm. How you respond at this early stage will help when the time comes to prepare them to move on.

You should always be open and honest, while addressing their anxieties. It is important to acknowledge that you cannot give a definitive answer to many of their questions. Explain that your job is to make sure that they are happy and well looked after at home. Reassure them by saying that everyone (including their mum and dad, if appropriate) is working hard to find them somewhere nice to live.

Encourage children to talk to their social worker about their concerns for the future. Co-ordinate with their social worker to make sure that you use similar language. Record what children say about what *they* want to happen in your diary notes, as it will inform their care plan.

We are always open about what short-term foster care means. We explain that children come to stay with us while social workers work with their families to decide what is best for them. We tell them about other children who lived with us in the past and are now happy in their new homes. We are fortunate in being able to introduce some of them, so they can see how happy they are. This also shows that we remain a part of our foster children's lives, even after they have moved on.

No matter how discreet you are, children and young people have an uncanny sense that something has changed when the focus of the placement shifts to permanency. The tone of conversations is different, new people and new names enter the conversation. This is why it is best to be as open as you can as proceedings unfold.

A child's behaviour can regress at this stage. Be prepared for an increase in arguments and tantrums. It is a natural, instinctive response to deep anxiety about the future.

The ideal situation is that when a final decision is made it does not come as a surprise to the children, but is the obvious outcome to a process that has included them and taken their views into account.

Meeting their new families

When your foster child moves on, there are four options for permanency: a return to the family home; placement with a member of the extended family (via a special guardianship order); long-term foster care; and adoption. Each outcome will impose different demands on you as a foster carer, although, ultimately, saying goodbye to your foster child will leave a sense of loss.

Returning home

The most common outcome for children in care is returning home to a parent or relative. This takes place after a comprehensive risk assessment to reassure the family court that such a course of action is safe and is in a child's best interests. The return is usually conditional on significant support being put in place for the family and continued assessment to ensure that children are living in a safe environment.

Many children are delighted to be reunited with their parents and are excited to be returning to their family home. Their return is usually preceded by an increase in the frequency of parental contact sessions, and home visits to gradually reintroduce them to home life.

However, some children and young people experience severe anxiety at the prospect of returning to a home where they have suffered abuse or neglect. In some cases, they will feel let down by a system that appears to have done little to protect them. A further concern will be the ability of children to readjust to a standard of living that may be lower than they have experienced during their time in care.

As a foster carer, you will need to work with the fostering team to reassure your foster child that the source of danger (for example, an abusive father or partner) has been removed and will not return. Together, you may need to demonstrate that the mother is now able to care for her children. Show what support is now in place. Identify people (such as a social worker or teacher) who they can raise concerns with after they have returned home.

If appropriate, visit their home so that they can show you around, which can help create a link for them between their family home and their foster home. You may also be able to be included in the support plan agreed with the family court, which will reassure the children and enable you to continue to be part of their lives.

Special guardianships

A foster child may be approved by the family court to live with a member of the extended family, typically a grandparent, aunt or older sibling. This is likely to be facilitated via a special guardianship order (see Chapter 11). This arrangement has the advantage of enabling a child to grow up within their own family in an environment that is judged to be safe and stable. Custody can be granted to a family member who has little or no previous connection to the child.

As above, contact between you and your foster child is likely to be severely restricted for the first few weeks. This period may be extended if it is judged that the child needs longer to settle.

You may have the opportunity to get to know the eventual guardian while the child is in placement. You should bear in mind that if a special guardianship order is an option, there may be more than one relative seeking custody, which can cause friction within the family. They may seek to encourage friendship with you in the hope of influencing the eventual outcome. It is important not to show any preference, particularly if you wish to maintain a continuing relationship with the child.

Once a decision is taken regarding your foster child's guardian, there will be a transitional period when they will spend time together, initially in your home before gradually moving to their permanent home. The timing will depend on how well the child already knows the relative and the home, but once the child has been told, it is important for the move to take place swiftly to avoid further uncertainty or upset.

Long-term foster care

This can be one of the most difficult transitions to manage. For a child or young person, a move to long-term foster care is confirmation that no family member was willing or able to provide a home, particularly if this is what they had hoped for. They may also feel rejected by you, as they are forced to move from one foster carer to another. It can be particularly dispiriting for the foster child or young person if they are moving outside the local area, which involves changing schools (again) and making new friends (again). Contact between you and your former foster child will be discouraged for the first few weeks.

Adoption

Although adoption is widely regarded as the ideal outcome for looked-after children, the reality is that relatively few (about 4%) are adopted. Most children are adopted between the ages of one and four, and the likelihood of adoption falls quickly after a child's fourth birthday. Because of the procedural complexities (generally, all other options are ruled out first), a child destined for adoption is likely to remain in care with you for longer than children identified for other long-term outcomes. This means that for many of these children the foster family is the only home they can remember.

The transition period, after the child is introduced to the adoptive parents, can be intense, not least because of the emotional commitment that the parents are making. In many cases, the adoptive parents will not have met the child until the first encounter in your home, and will know the child only through case notes and photographs. They have probably been waiting years for this moment. The pressure on them (and you) to establish a bond with the child over a relatively small period is immense. In cases involving the youngest children, the adoptive parents will spend several days at your home, from first thing in the morning until last thing at night, and will share the routine with you, including tasks like bath time, nappy changes and feeding. You will reciprocate, spending time with the child at their home, before gradually moving into the background as a prelude to letting go.

Both of you will have the child's best interests at heart, but you may come from different backgrounds and have different ideas about how tasks should be carried out, based on your own lifetime experiences. It takes great skill as a foster carer to maintain a positive outlook throughout this intense period, and you are likely to feel emotionally drained at the end of each day.

The ambition is to make the move as seamless as possible for the child, and this will be best achieved if there is a harmonious relationship between carer and adoptive parent. Be as kind as you can to each other. The chances are that you are all feeling raw.

Continuing contact with foster children

When a placement comes to an end, foster carers have limited control over further contact with their foster child. In fact, there is a system-wide presumption that a 'clean break' is usually in a child's best interests. This is applied most rigorously in cases of adoption, when the priority is for adoptive families to be given time and space to bond. But it is likely also to apply to children who move to long-term foster care or are subjects of special guardianship orders. Contact will be at the discretion of the child's new carers or guardians, and they are likely to be advised by their social workers to wait. This can mean that foster carers often must wait for several weeks, and sometimes months, to receive news about how the child is coping with the move.

Of course, not all foster carers feel the need to stay in contact with foster children, particularly if the placement has been difficult or ended suddenly. But many foster carers do find the lack of contact and information unsettling, and it can be bewildering for their own children. To the foster carer, it can appear cruel and even inhumane. You will feel vulnerable at a time when any support you have had is withdrawn as the placement comes to an end.

How you cope with this aspect of the job may well determine your longevity as a foster carer. There is no single coping strategy guaranteed to help you and your family, and the end of each placement will have a different effect on you. Here are some coping strategies that have helped our family:

- Work as a team. Try not to overwhelm the next carer with information. Suggest, rather than instruct. Be aware of their anxieties. Accept that they will have different views. Respect these differences.

- Stress your commitment to doing what is best for the child. Make it clear that you always are available to help, whether it is by email, letter or phone call.

- Spare no effort in preparing the child's memory book and memory box. These are vivid reminders of how much love you have given your foster child, and how much you care.

- Don't expect too much. You may part on the best of terms, promising to be lifelong friends, only to subsequently hear that they wish to have only limited contact.

- Play the long game. Don't try to fight the system, because it always gives the impression that you are thinking of your own feelings rather than the child's. Be patient. As adoptive parents or long-term carers gain in confidence, it will be easier for them to get in touch.

- Remember key dates. Send cards or token gifts on birthdays and at Christmas and Easter. The first day at school is also important. Make a note of adoptive parents' birthdays and significant anniversaries. Don't expect an acknowledgement, but be pleasantly surprised if and when you do hear back.

- Seek support from other foster carers. You are not alone; every foster carer has a positive and a negative story to tell.

- Remember how amazing you are – you have changed a child's life. Nobody can take that away from you. You have precious memories that nobody can ever take away.

When a foster child leaves, you also say goodbye to a broad community of people who have been such an important part of your life for the duration of the placement. The child's social work team quickly disperses to focus on the many other cases in a bulging in-tray. You will no longer be doing the school run or trip to the nursery. That means bidding farewell to the teachers and support staff who have made your foster child so welcome in class, providing the additional support that was so desperately needed.

It also means saying goodbye to the mums and dads of your foster child's classmates, whom you have come to know so well. You may have spent time in each other's homes, and helped to ferry each other's children to and from school and to after-school activities. There will be many contacts on your mobile phone who you will never phone again.

You will hope to keep in touch, but it is difficult once your foster child has left, severing the most important (and possibly only) connection. Your next placement will introduce you to a new school, and a new cohort of teachers and parents. The emotional investment you must make on behalf of your next foster child makes continued engagement with people from your previous placement extremely difficult. There is only so much of you to go around.

This may seem obvious, and unavoidable. But that does not make it any easier. This is why it is so important to maintain friendships and interests that have no connection to fostering. These are people who know you, and value your friendship because of who you are, rather than because you are a foster carer. Cherish those relationships. Much as you love and care for your foster children, they are likely one day to leave you, and you must be prepared for that. By looking after yourself (physically and emotionally) you will be a better carer for your children.

A placement may come to a sudden end if there is a breakdown in trust between the carer and the foster child or young person. Sometimes the physical and emotional burden of care becomes unsustainable. A decision to end a placement is not taken lightly and will follow extensive consultation with the many stakeholders involved in a child's care. Additional support can be put in place to enable the placement to continue, but there will be cases when this is not enough, and it is in the best interests of both the child and the foster carer to make alternative arrangements for care.

The breakdown of a placement can be traumatic for the foster carer, as well as for the child. It raises questions about your ability as a foster carer and can seriously undermine your confidence. In the worst-case scenario, you may decide not to foster again.

The reasons for the breakdown of a placement are complex, and it is important for a review of each case to consider what lessons can be learned. But the reality is that, from time to time, placements will fail. Personalities clash; the changing demands and requirements of a vulnerable child or young person are difficult to manage; the support available may not be adequate. Foster carers need to be honest with themselves about their abilities, and not be afraid to admit that a placement has become too challenging. The interests of a child are paramount, but a foster carer must never put their own health and well-being at risk.

Take a break; be kind to yourself and to your loved ones. Move on.

Between placements

We try to take a break between placements. This can range from a few weeks to a couple of months, depending on how we feel after a child leaves. Ideally, we take a holiday away from home to get a complete change of scene.

We treat ourselves and our daughters to a special dinner to celebrate the completion of the placement, and to thank them for the enormous contribution they make to foster care.

Take the opportunity to spend time with close friends and family, who inevitably are neglected when you are fostering. Even those you see regularly will appreciate spending time with you, without children. Now is the time to do some of those things you are unable to contemplate when you have foster children.

It is a good time to tackle home maintenance. Foster care causes significant wear and tear on the home, which is easier to put right when there are no children around. Chances are, you have also been putting off medical and dental appointments because you were so busy. Make sure that check-ups are close to the top of your 'to do' list.

Footnote

We remain in touch with all the children we have fostered. Some we see regularly, others occasionally. All the children are doing well.

At Christmas, we hosted a party attended by ten of 'our' children and their parents or carers, who have all become friends. We hope they will come back in the spring for an Easter Egg hunt. These are joyous, family occasions, also attended by our daughters and, these days, our grandson.

These gatherings are also a comfort to our current foster children, who benefit from the friendship of boys and girls who share a lived experience of what they are going through. They can see what their future might look like.

We know that we are fortunate to be in this position. It reflects, in no small part, the human quality of the carers who followed us in the children's lives. But these relationships are rooted in connections made early in the placement, when the focus was still on managing crisis, and not yet on considering outcomes.

At the heart of this engagement is an acknowledgement that families in crisis are families just like ours, and yours. We work with mums and dads and grandparents whose life stories might easily be ours. We support children with the same dreams our girls had when they were growing up.

A lesson of foster care is that the margin between happiness and tragedy, and between fulfilment and disappointment, is very thin indeed.

CASE STUDY

The end of placement by definition should signify the finish of…the conclusion of…the termination of…the final part.

However, feelings and thoughts are a never-ending part of our human existence. Therefore, for myself and many foster carers who welcome children into our lives, often in or after very difficult circumstances, and then say goodbye, we sometimes wish things were different, that we had been listened to…we sometimes wish we had listened more…we sometimes wish we had hung in there…we sometimes think 'good grief, how did we manage that?'…and we sometimes realise that a child needs more than our family is able to offer at that time.

Our thoughts help us to reflect – to take time, to recover and to learn from each experience – and as each placement is different in time, emotion and experience, the collating, reflecting and healing is different each time. Sometimes we wish we had been told more – would it have been different then? Sometimes we think, what a great result, how wonderful that we got them through that. Sometimes we are able to keep in touch, to help, to see them happy. Sometimes we wonder: Are you okay? Where are you now? Did you keep up the football? The guitar? The dance classes? The horse riding? Did you realise those dreams?

Most of all we are always remembering. You see, memories do not end…feelings and thoughts never end.

As I put up our Christmas tree, there are all the handmade decorations that the children have made with me – memories of each Christmas with each child, sprinkling fairy dust in the bushes, making a sweetie house, visiting Santa, making nativity costumes, and the thousands of things that foster carers do that bond and make memories, with all the emotions that go with them. How they responded…how we were together…

My chipped elephant ornament sits on the windowsill, bought for me at a boot sale with my foster daughter's pocket money, and in the child's own words, 'Because Auntie likes elephants because they never forget.' Well, it's like us foster carers, isn't it? Every day I look at that elephant and every day I remember her. When I forget it will be when I am in my nursing home robbed of my memories, and that will be sad.

It doesn't end for our family members either. My son has his memories; my mum too, who every Pancake Day showed the children how to make and flip a pancake, becomes emotional…of course, we all do, we are human.

This is why keeping a record of the child's life with us is so important; they need those memories too, and sometimes when they struggle emotionally, mentally or just through being so young, the memories can get lost. It is important that a child has a record. At the end of a placement for two sisters, one of them said, 'I am worried you will forget me', and the other said, 'You know I can't remember things well; what if I forget?' Having their life book reassured them.

Every placement is different, with some more difficult emotionally than others. For us, it is knowing that in the more difficult ones we gave everything we had to give, and sometimes the decisions that were made were beyond our control.

At these times it is comforting to know that you have support from your supervising social worker and other staff members, that you are allowed to have time to come to terms with things, so that you can grieve, heal, reflect, learn and be in a better place to help another child or young person. It helps to have time with family, good friends and other foster carers who have an understanding of your sense of loss and grief.

It's important to know and take comfort from the fact that the efforts we, our family and friends have made will effect change and be rewarded in the future, as the child or young person will have more of an understanding of a happy and stable family life and friendships and what they want for their own family. It is joyful when you realise and are told later by the child how important their time was with you.

Who would have thought the first child ever placed with us 17 years ago, who spent months with us enjoying playing hairdressers with a doll's head, an old hairdryer missing its lead and a pile of hair clips and bands, with me and other family members becoming her clients, would now be a hairdresser?

In our last placement, the child caught up on years of school work and no longer needed a support assistant, meaning that she could be in mainstream secondary school and embark on her GCSEs. We helped her learn to play, socialise and make friends. Her future is changed, it's brighter and it's better, and that's what gets us through and makes us want to help another child.

So as I see it, fostering placements never 'end', they just become part of who we are.

CASE STUDY

The one part of fostering we were not prepared for was having to say goodbye for the first time. It was a difficult situation as the ten-year-old girl (who I will refer to as G we were fostering had a good relationship with my husband Rod, but not with me. We never really knew the reason for this, just that mum was very rarely on the scene and contact was almost zero, whereas dad had regular contact, and it may be that G just felt closer to males. She always looked for affection from Rod but never looked for any from me. She just constantly said black if I said white! To say this was difficult was an understatement, and it got to the point that the whole situation was affecting us as a couple (something we had both agreed we would never allow to happen). G would behave one way with me, but as soon as Rod came home she was a completely different child. I sometimes felt as though Rod thought I was imagining her challenging behaviour. We took the very hard decision to end the placement and were very fortunate in that the charity we foster for were incredibly supportive and managed to find another carer for G (and where she remains 20 months later).

Those few days between telling G she was moving and her actually moving were very difficult. We did our best to explain the reasons for it, but G never said much, until the night before she moved. We went to bed and she had left a letter for us telling us we were the best carers she had had and she would always love us. I think it's the only time we have cried together during our fostering journey (who knows if it will be the last!).

The day G left will stay with me forever. She was fine all morning until her social worker arrived, and then she hid under the bed. I distinctly remember the fear written all over her face as she started to panic. As I did not have a very close relationship with G, I thought it would be easy to say goodbye, but as soon as I did so, the tears came and we were all crying. Once we had waved goodbye I felt a huge sense of relief (which made me feel even more guilty), but I was acutely aware that Rod was devastated. I had to support him knowing that I was responsible for how he was feeling, which was hard, but we do everything regarding fostering as a team and I knew he did not blame me in any way. We still get regular updates about G via our supervising social worker and also from her new foster carer via social media, which has helped us accept that we made the best decision for her. We did our bit for G, and I know her time here benefited her, and I now feel much less guilty. It was extremely hard at the time as, with it being our first placement, we felt as if we had failed. I think it's crucial for foster carers to know at the beginning of a placement never to feel disheartened if things go wrong. Unfortunately, it happens, and as much as we have to do what's right for the child, sometimes we have to do what's right for us as a family too.

CASE STUDY

We began fostering in 2012. Our first placement was a newborn premature baby, who came to us when she was only a few hours old. She was tiny and needed to be fed a special formula. We soon formed a great bond with her and she had positive routines. However, without warning, after a month the local authority decided to move the baby to an in-house placement. We only had three hours' notice to prepare. We thought we had done something wrong, but there were no concerns regarding the care the baby received from us, as the local authority placed another baby with us a week later!

As you can imagine, this was a very traumatic ending as there was not enough time to prepare ourselves or our family to say goodbye. No discussions were had with the new carer and so no routines were shared. I was so angry with the local authority I told the local authority social worker that she was not doing her job properly!

It was disgusting how they moved her as she was so settled with us. Of course, all of the equipment and clothing we had bought for her went with her to her new placement.

Sadly, there are times when you have to question if the decision being made for the child is in the child's best interests or driven by finance. This was our introduction to fostering and placement endings.

Our second placement was a three-day-old baby with foetal alcohol syndrome. We remember collecting him from the hospital. He had developmental delay and there were many health issues and appointments for us to keep with him. This baby stayed with us for nine months before being adopted by the adoptive parents of his half-sister. This was a good outcome, but we found this the most difficult ending of all. We had formed a very close bond with the baby and found it incredibly difficult to let him go to his new home. We were given the opportunity to apply to adopt the baby, 'first refusal' if you like, but we felt that we did not have the finances to meet his lifelong care needs that this other couple were better placed to do so. We still both feel upset when we think about it now, several years on.

Unlike our first baby placement, this baby had a planned transition over a two-week period. The adopt-ive couple lived a significant distance from our home, and so the introductions and transition of care was done gradually at our address. We included the adoptive parents in all aspects of the baby's care, and they attended all health appointments with us so that they could familiarise themselves with his health needs.

The baby did not take to them at first as he had formed a strong attachment to us (especially the male carer) and would cry when this carer was no longer in sight.

Due to his health needs and the stiffness of his body, he was more difficult to hold and cuddle and it was more difficult to console him when he became distressed. It could not have been easy for the new adoptive parents who needed to be very patient and consistent with him.

We knew that we had to step back, practically and emotionally. It was very difficult to hold our emotions in, in front of the adoptive parents. We knew it was the best thing for the baby and his future needs to go to them as he was to be adopted with his half-sibling. His adoptive parents could afford private tuition for him and were in a much better place financially to meet his needs. We instantly fell apart when he left us, and we grieved deeply for him.

Initially we did contact the adoptive parents and sent a birthday card and they sent back a photo, but they did not want ongoing contact or any reminder that he had been in our care. They just wanted to be a 'normal family'. We needed to respect this.

Our next placement to arrive was a teenage girl aged 15 years. This was a totally different fostering experience after caring for babies, and initially we welcomed the change – until we experienced her challenging behaviours. This placement lasted for six months, but it felt much longer with it being our first experience of caring for a teenager. We enjoyed spending time together having 'girlie sessions', doing nails and hair and, of course, shopping. Our young son, because of his age, did not relate much to the young person in placement. All went well until she discovered boys and had a boyfriend. The boyfriend soon became far more important than we were. She detached herself from family life, and just as she was about to come on holiday abroad with us, she refused to come. Also, her behaviour towards us became increasingly hostile, with her threatening to make allegations, being aggressive and making threats to self-harm, and so with the welfare of the family to consider, we gave notice on the placement. Just before we left for a holiday, she moved into a residential unit. We took her and helped her unpack and settle in. When we returned from holiday, she asked if she could come back to live with us, but we felt that this was too much of a risk. However, she has been a frequent visitor to our home since. Our door is always open to her and she can contact us for advice and support at any time. We try to encourage her and congratulate her on any achievements, however small. On reflection, we do not regret saying to her that she could not return as it was the correct decision for our family at that time. There is certainly no bad feeling between us and we enjoy staying in touch with her.

Before this placement ended, we were offered care of another baby. Looking back, we do not think that the young girl liked sharing our attention.

This baby came to us at five months old with a skull fracture in two places, and he left just after his first birthday. We did not know if he would have developmental delay or a learning disability from this injury, which was said to be non-accidental. He had scans every two months and thankfully was meeting his developmental milestones. The care plan for him was to be twin-tracked for adoption or returning home. We felt very privileged caring for this baby as we had the joy of being there for his first milestones, first words, first steps and first foods, and we enjoyed a very close bond with him. Our son also enjoyed having him as part of the family and spent a lot of time interacting with him.

We knew that the baby could return to his mum and so we worked as closely as we could with her. We set up a contact book and would write to her to tell her about her baby's progress. This became a useful tool of communication and helped the mother to feel included in his life. It also contributed towards the child's life story/memory box.

As time progressed, we took on the responsibility of taking the baby for contact sessions to see his mother. This gave us the opportunity to get to know and understand her and gave her the opportunity to learn from us in how we met the baby's needs. We made sure that his mother was invited to all health appointments and helped her to understand what had been said. We kept in direct contact over the phone and kept her updated with the baby's progress, keeping her involved and feeling part of his life, but we did not feel it appropriate to use social media with her.

The transition plan to return the baby to his mother was over a four-week period. We began by welcoming her into our home to spend time with us and the baby and to share meals, giving her time to observe and learn and ask questions. We recognised that she was young and vulnerable and had been in a difficult relationship and she did not pose any risk to us.

The next step was for us to take the baby to his mum's home, spend a few hours there and stay for dinner. Then we took him to her home and left him in her care for a few hours before collecting him. The plan progressed to an overnight stay for the baby at the mother's home. Working so closely with her made the transition easier, as we could see the baby was being looked after appropriately and was happy in his mother's care, especially as her confidence grew. She felt comfortable enough to ask us lots of questions and she did not pretend to know everything. We could tell that she was committed to being a good mum and asked us about his routines, his likes and dislikes, asking about the washing powder we used and introducing this into her own caring routine for the baby. Once the baby had returned to his mother full time, she felt able to contact us for advice and support, such as dealing with nappy rash or behavioural concerns. It was difficult explaining to our son that the baby was not coming back to us. He kept asking where the baby was and when he would be coming back. Our son has had to learn that the children who stay with us 'come and go'.

We are still in contact with the baby and his mum today. She knows that she is welcome in our home, and on his second birthday, she brought him over to see us and spent the day with us, which was a lovely surprise.

Our next placement was a 15-year-old girl who settled well in placement for the first six months. She was a bridesmaid at our wedding and related well to our family. However, once she was told that police were not going to prosecute an alleged abuser for sexual abuse against her, she began to give up on the placement and looked to return home to be with her mother and friends.

Whatever we did, we could not get her to attend school, either a local one or her previous school near her home, which she wanted to do. Her mother felt that she could not cope with her daughter returning home. Her daughter blamed us for keeping her in care. When she reached her 16th birthday, she wanted to return to her home area and often failed to return to us after contact and school. She thought that she could look after herself and no longer accepted our care. Her mother agreed for her to stay with her for Christmas, and she never came back to us. Sadly, there was no transition plan or a chance for a positive ending.

We have kept in touch with her and tried to encourage her. She was very bright and able to achieve good grades, but things did not work out for her with her mum and she did not return to education. We worry about her.

Our current placement is an unaccompanied asylum seeker who came to us at 17, looking more like a 13-year-old at the time. He is fantastic to have as part of the family, so much so that we are moving on to Staying Put with him as we are committed to him for as long as he needs us to be. This means that our fostering career will be on hold until he moves on, as we do not have the space for another foster child. We want to do this as he has lived most of his life on his own and has no one else, and it would not be fair to take this family away from him. He is not ready to live independently. His immigration status is not yet secure and we cannot let him deal with this uncertainty on his own.

It is scary for us to not foster and to get a lower income on Staying Put but we are doing this for him. He is good for us as well. He is part of our family, our boy. Our son sees him as a brother. He tries hard in his education, which is a breath of fresh air to us, and it is nice to feel proud of him. He is our forever kid. If he had come to us at a younger age, we would have adopted him. So for now, Staying Put is our own ending, until we can return to being foster carers.

When a placement is coming to an end we begin to distance ourselves in our own mind and you need to tell yourself that, in a few weeks, I will not be caring for this child. At least with some of the children we had time to prepare our family for the change, but when the endings come, you do grieve for them and hope that things will work out for them in their new homes. It is hard. You hope that they will be happy. It is difficult when you can't keep in touch and you feel blind not knowing how they are doing, and so keeping in touch is very helpful, for us and for the children and young people. We have got better at keeping in touch with people through experience.

There is a grieving process that you each have to manage. I find it easier if I keep busy. You have to get over it. We are in contact with the other placements and can find out how the children are, so that is good.

When the children leave us, we do 'have our wobbles', but we are able to bounce off one another and support one another. We do not seem to grieve at the same time or in the same way. I grieve straightaway and my partner remains strong. When I feel strong, he then shows his grief; however, when the second baby left, we were both in bits instantly! Our area manager from the fostering agency was very supportive, which was great.

The hardest part of fostering is when the children leave, however they leave.

Ending survival tips

- Whether you like the parents or not, you have to 'put a face on' and be professional for the child's sake. Even if you feel that you wouldn't let them look after your cat!

- Be open and friendly, so that they can approach you and keep in touch and feel able to ask advice.

- When a child moves on, make sure you have people around who you can speak to afterwards. Don't bottle it up. You have lost a child and you miss them.

- Prepare your birth children for the foster child leaving as it affects them too.

- Let the child take familiar things with them, such as a blanket. Let them sleep with it for several nights before they leave. Don't wash it, as it needs to have a familiar smell to help them settle. Even our 16-year-old took a blanket with her.

- During the placement, take plenty of photos of everything and keep digital copies. Use them for the child's memory book.

- You have to remind yourself that they are not yours as you lead up to them leaving, as hard as that is. It is your place to look after them for a while and it is not necessarily permanent.

- Keep in touch whenever possible as this benefits the kids and you. If this is not possible, you have to let go and not hold grudges. Any contact is a blessing with all of them. If they call round, always make them welcome, no matter how inconvenient it may be.

- Remember the good times. When teenagers have left, it has been a relief at first, but after a while you have to let the bad things go and remember the positives and all of the good times you had with them.

- Leave the door open in your relationship so that people can stay in touch, no matter what they have done.

- Respect their choice to leave.

Conclusion

Endings and goodbyes are very, very tough. There's no getting around it, there is no avoiding them. This is a process that you are going to go through as a foster carer, and while this chapter may have prepared you for what's coming and given you some valuable insights from foster carers into how they've managed to cope with endings, you are going to feel goodbyes emotionally and this is going to be hard. Seek support from your social worker, fellow foster carers, friends and family. Don't try and block out the emotions you feel; accept them and work through them. The goodbyes are unlikely to become any easier as you continue through your fostering career, but you will gain perspective and that is a very valuable thing. When it is possible to stay in touch, do so. Seeing what your child has gone on to achieve is one of the joys of foster care.

Chapter 14

'HEROES OF THE STATE' – THE DIFFERENCE FOSTERING CAN MAKE

—— Andy Elvin and Martin Barrow ——

So yes we are fostered
And when I say this the lines on people's faces crumble up
    like discarded pages of paper laden with mistakes
But we are not mistakes on pages
We are simply awesome novels
With unorthodox beginnings

We are not mistakes on pages
We are simply a crooked introduction straightened out by
    proofreaders Pat and Vic
Whose love and guidance set the foundations for straight
    lines for us to write the rest of our story on
No we are not mistakes on pages

Solomon OB

'Before I came into care I missed a lot of education. I used to live in hostels with my mum and moved around a lot. My attendance has been good since I've been in foster care.'

'I never felt safe at home but I always feel safe in my foster home.'

'I like my foster home because I've had a better life and I've made lots of progress at school. There were always lots of arguments at home and there aren't any here.'

As we said in the introduction, Lord Laming recently called foster carers 'Heroes of the State', and so they are. Foster care is an almost unique role within the UK, and every day in every way foster carers all around the UK are improving the lives of vulnerable children.

Good foster care can make a transformative difference to a child's life. There are over 70,000 children in foster care in the UK, and there is always a need for more foster carers to come forward to care for these vulnerable children, especially those who wish to care for teenage children.

CASE STUDY

I had always thought of fostering having raised my three sons, but my husband wasn't keen on the idea, feeling that we had done our bit. I had become a widow in 2012 and remarried in 2014, but it only lasted a year. I lost Dad in 2015 and felt at a loose end with my life. My children were all grown up in their 30s with children of their own. It was my time to do something that I had always dreamed of.

I had previously worked with vulnerable teenagers and had always wanted to do more to help them; an agency was recommended to me and I contacted them in May 2015. The process is lengthy, but I can honestly say I learned a great deal about myself going through it. I really enjoyed it and developed a good relationship with my social worker. I went to panel in the October and actually cried during the process as it meant so much to me to be approved.

In January I had my first referral, 14-year-old Ellie. She was a planned move, which meant we could get to know each other before she came to live with me in February 2016 with her two rabbits. Sadly, Ellie's mum had died in 2012, she had no contact with her dad and I was her fifth foster carer placement.

I had my second referral in May, a girl aged 12 on a respite placement for three weeks. And then in November I had a referral for a 17-year-old girl who, happily, continues to live with us.

During the summer Ellie and I went on holiday to Mexico and then to visit my eldest son in Canada. She fulfilled her dream of swimming with dolphins while we were in Mexico. We felt like a real family unit and the rest of my family could not have been more welcoming, which is important as it does involve all of us.

It's lovely to have teenagers in the house again. I have lost my nice, tidy, quiet home, but I wouldn't swap it – I love the atmosphere.

I found myself really looking forward to Christmas as the previous year I woke up on Christmas morning by myself and this year it was going to be with two very excited young ladies. We got the Christmas Eve boxes ready, and the Christmas bedding. We are very family orientated, and the girls saved their pocket money to buy presents.

They were both excited to be with me for Christmas, but obviously there was sadness also, as they were not with their families. We seem to blend really well together. Ellie is doing very well at school and the older girl is at college; both girls help me around the house and we cook together.

Our Christmas Day started with the presents and a lovely breakfast before visiting family to give our presents out, then home for lunch and to watch a Christmas movie. The highlight for the girls was opening the new phones they both have asked for. For me it was watching their faces as they open their presents, and knowing I'm doing my little bit to make things better for them. I love them.

There is often a mistaken belief that foster care is somehow temporary and does not offer a permanent home or relationship to a child. This is simply not the case. Though some fostering placements, by design, may be short, many are long term, and the relationship between the child and their foster parents is lifelong. Many foster carers go on to be grandparents for their foster children's children, and many foster fathers have given away their foster daughters on their wedding day. Children who have been in care often turn to their foster family when they want to share significant milestones in their adult life.

With the advent of Staying Put, many young people will remain in their foster families until they are 21. More and more foster families are gaining special guardianship orders in respect of their foster children, so becoming their legal guardians.

Many foster families get together with the children they have cared for on occasions such as Christmas and birthdays, or they hold an annual summer get-together.

All of the above replicates how families in the general population behave. Foster families are, first and foremost, families. They are there to care for, teach, support and love the children and young people who join their families. They ensure that these young people have an opportunity to recover from traumatic experiences and go on to lead successful and happy adult lives.

Though many placements may be presented to you as being short term, the very nature of children's social care means that you can never tell. There are countless examples of children who were placed in an emergency with a plan for the placement only to last a few weeks and then those children stay with their foster family until they leave home.

Though the media can seem to be full of stories about the poor outcomes for children who have been in care, these stories are often partial and do not reflect the reality lived by the majority of children in care. Those children who have long-term, stable foster placements can and do go on to achieve very positive outcomes that are broadly in line with children who are not in care. Yes, there is more to achieve; we need more young people from foster care to go on to university and into apprenticeships, and we need the government to support this by offering free tuition fees or a guaranteed apprenticeship for all children who leave care.

CASE STUDY

For many young people, university will be the first time that they've left home to live independently. It'll be a pivotal moment in their lives, leaving their family and friends to pursue higher education. It will end in a degree that will make or break whether or not they reach their dream career.

But for foster children, that dream seems much more far off than for others. Only 6% of children in the fostering system make it to university. A lot of people might argue that most foster children are lazy and will never amount to anything, that they misbehave and therefore will not provide the grades for a successful application.

However, some children in the care system want more out of life, to break the stereotypes that they are bound by. But when they've lived life hearing that children in their position are less likely to do well, it becomes a self-fulfilling prophecy. If they believe they will do badly, they will.

That's what I did, at first. I had spent years watching crime shows where almost all of the criminals were portrayed as people who had spent their childhoods in and out of foster care, and then turned to a life of crime.

I reached 17 years old and was almost scared to submit an application. All my friends were in the process of choosing what locations and courses they wanted to apply for, whereas I was stuck questioning whether or not it was worth it.

I was just another care kid who would never be successful. My dreams were just that – fantasies that would never become real.

It took a couple of pep talks from various teachers and Lynne, my foster carer, before I even entertained the idea. I submitted an application to my university of choice, did two interviews for two courses and a joint honours, and then finished my A-levels. I spent the summer worrying about what I was supposed to do with my life if I didn't get into university.

I needn't have worried. On the day that I was to go and pick up my A-level results, I received an email. I was with my boyfriend, just scrolling through my laptop, and I must have frightened him to death, because I suddenly burst into tears.

All I could say was 'I got in!' and then I attracted the rest of the household, who all congratulated me and said that they knew I could do it. Next I called Lynne, who cheered down the phone with me and was ready with a congratulations card when she picked me up from results day.

I felt a bit ashamed of myself for a while afterwards for not believing in myself more.

Why didn't I believe that I could get in? I was just as able as any other person my age. Starting university, I was afraid that people would see me differently if I admitted that I was in foster care. Yet again, I needn't have worried, as all of my peers were accepting and treated me as they did everyone else. The only difference was that my lecturers were a bit more wary of how they treated me. I was often called into their office for 'meetings', with them patronisingly asking how I was doing, but this soon stopped when they realised that I wasn't handling the course any better or worse than the rest of my classmates.

At the end of the day, I am still human. I am still just a teenager tackling the difficulties of university like any other. The only difference between my uni friends and me is that I don't call my parental figures 'Mum' and 'Dad'.

Conclusion

Fostering can be tough – it will probably be the most challenging role you ever take up, but it will also be the most life affirming and the most rewarding.

It is not just a child whose life is transformed. Your life, and that of your family, will change forever. So do not enter into fostering lightly or on a whim but know that, when you do, you will not be taking the journey alone and your fostering agency or local authority will be there to support you every step of the way. It is a truism that it takes a village to raise a child, and fostering reinforces this.

By offering a secure, safe, loving and stable home you can be the catalyst that transforms a child's difficult early life into a happy childhood and a successful adult life.

We hope that this book has inspired you to pick up the phone or type 'how to become a foster carer' into your search engine and to begin your fostering story.

The Foster Carers' Charter

This is for every foster carer in the UK and outlines what your rights and responsibilities are.

Roles and commitment

The fostering service's role

The fostering service aims to provide stable and first-rate foster care for children who are valued, supported and encouraged to grow and develop as individuals. To achieve this aim, we recruit, train and approve foster carers and deliver ongoing support to them.

Foster carers' role

Foster carers are at the heart of the foster care service. We are assessed, trained and supported to look after children and young people in a family environment, providing them with stability, care and an opportunity to grow and develop and to reach their potential.

Our working relationships are based on mutual trust and respect. This charter explains what we expect from each other.

The fostering service's commitment – you can expect from us:

- working in partnership
- full information
- clarity about decisions
- support

- learning and development
- fair treatment
- communication and consultation.

Foster carers' commitment – you can expect from us:

- working in partnership
- respect for the child
- sharing of information
- learning, development and support
- communication and consultation.

What foster carers can expect from the fostering service

1 Working in partnership

We recognise that foster carers have skills and expertise and make the biggest difference to the everyday lives of children in care. We will:

- value your skills and expertise equally to those of other professionals
- recognise that you are the people who live with children every day and know them best
- include you in all meetings that affect you and the children you care for
- ensure that our fostering service will meet the standards set out in fostering regulations and guidance
- treat you without discrimination and respect you as a colleague
- respect confidentiality.

2 Full information

We know that information is vital in order for foster carers to provide care that meets the child's need. We will:

- give you all the information you need in order to care safely for the child

- provide this information in writing prior to placement (except when there are emergency placements and it is not feasible to do so, but we will provide this information as soon as possible)

- ensure that there is a placement plan drawn up in discussion with you and agreed with you in advance of placements (except in emergencies where this will be done as soon as possible)

- provide you with information on all financial matters including tax, allowances and additional entitlements

- provide you with full details of all relevant departmental policies and procedures.

3 Clarity about decisions

We recognise that in order for children to live a full family life foster carers must be able to make decisions regarding the children they foster. We will:

- ensure that, wherever possible, you are able to make everyday decisions that mean that your fostered child is not treated differently to their peers and can feel part of your family

- provide clarity about any decision you cannot take at the outset so that everyone understands who is responsible for what.

4 Support

We recognise that fostering can be an isolating and challenging task and that appropriate and timely support makes all the difference to the fostering family and to the child in your care. We will:

- respond positively to requests for additional support

- provide you with at least monthly contact, bi-monthly supervision and weekly phone contact

- give you honest and open feedback

- provide you with access to 24-hour support from people with fostering expertise

- pay you allowances, expenses and fees in a timely manner

- pay fees that reflect the task

- ensure that there is a local group, recognised by the fostering service, where you and your family can find support and share experiences with other fostering families.

5 Learning and development

We believe that foster carers must be enabled to access learning and development opportunities throughout their fostering career. This will ensure they have the skills and knowledge they need, and allow them to develop their practice in order that they can help transform the lives of the children they foster. We will:

- provide you and your family with appropriate and relevant training by trainers who understand the fostering task

- enable you to access online training as needed

- provide you with other development opportunities which make the best use of your skills and expertise, such as mentoring or providing additional training or support.

6 *Fair treatment*

We recognise that foster carers have a right to be treated fairly, no matter what the circumstances. We will:

- consult with you before changing terms and conditions

- ensure openness in all of our discussions and communications with you

- ensure that you are treated with respect, kept informed and provided with emotional support should you be subject to an allegation

- provide a framework for dealing with allegations and adhere to our agreed timescales

- ensure that you know the arrangements for the payment of fees and allowances in the event that you are not able to foster while the subject of an allegation.

7 *Communication and consultation*

We believe that open and honest dialogue is the key to a good relationship. We will:

- facilitate regular communication between you, supervising social workers, managers and directors of service as needed

- ensure that we consult with you in a meaningful way on matters that affect you

- give you timely feedback from consultations.

What the fostering service can expect from foster carers

1 Working in partnership

We will demonstrate a high standard of care and conduct. We will:

- demonstrate our expertise and make use of our skills to the best of our ability

- provide children with an experience of family life

- attend meetings about the children and young people we care for

- work with the agencies involved with the child, such as school, health and religious establishments

- show a willingness to work with birth parents, the wider family and people significant in a child's life

- meet the standards set out in fostering regulations and guidance and follow departmental policies and procedures

- respect confidentiality.

2 Respect for the child

Every child and young person should be respected as an individual and be supported in meeting their needs and achieving their aspirations and potential. We will:

- respect and promote a child's religious, linguistic and cultural heritage

- afford the same level of protection and care to a child as we would our own child in accordance with the national minimum standards

- ensure the child has the right to make decisions regarding their own lives, as appropriate to their age and understanding.

3 Sharing of information

We believe that open and honest dialogue is the key to a good relationship. We will:

- inform our supervising social worker about changes in our household

- inform our supervising social worker about any difficulties that arise for us.

4 Learning, development and support

We must be enabled to access learning and development opportunities throughout our fostering career. This will ensure that we have the skills and knowledge we need, and allow us to develop our practice in order that we can help transform the lives of the children we foster. We will:

- be prepared to develop our skills throughout our fostering career

- attend relevant training

- take up opportunities offered to us such as online learning

- let you know if we are unable to attend

- attend and contribute to support groups.

5 Communication and consultation

We believe that open and honest dialogue is the key to a good relationship. We will:

- respond to local consultations, surveys and discussions in order to inform the development of the service

- meet with service managers, inspectors, researchers and others in order to promote dialogue and a good working relationship.

Contributors

Andy Elvin is CEO of TACT, the UK's largest dedicated fostering and adoption charity. He is a social worker and former foster carer. He was previously CEO of the Charity Children and Families Across Borders (CFAB). Andy was also a founding Trustee of the Social Work Charity Frontline.

Martin Barrow and his wife Lorna have been foster carers for eight years, specialising in sibling groups. They have two adult daughters and one grandson. Martin is a journalist and writer. You can read his Huffington Post blog about being a foster carer at http://www.huffingtonpost.co.uk/author/martin-barrow Martin lives in West Sussex.

Louise Cox has 18 years' experience working with children and young people in education, healthcare and statutory settings in the UK. Since qualifying in 2005 she has worked in foster care services as a supervising social worker and manager. Louise is currently working in Uganda for a child protection organisation specialising in deinstitutionalisation and alternative care.

Martin Clarke qualified as a Social Worker in 1980 and has since worked for the NSPCC, Action for Children, Derbyshire CC and Northamptonshire CC before joining TACT in 2005. He became TACT's Learning and Development Manager in 2007. Aside from work, Martin's main interests are his family (he has a son aged 18 and a daughter aged 13), real ale and sport...particularly Nottingham Panthers Ice Hockey Club!

Bev Pickering was an operational manager in a fostering team for 10 years. She is now the Business Development Director for TACT and her role encompasses the recruitment of carers, contract monitoring and performance and new area development. In addition to her fostering and adoption knowledge and experience, Bev has worked in a range of settings across adult and children's services.

Dr. John Simmonds is Director of Policy, Research and Development at CoramBAAF, formerly the British Association for Adoption and Fostering. He is a qualified social worker and has substantial experience in child protection, family placement and residential care settings. He is currently responsible for CoramBAAF's contribution to the development of policy and practice in social work, health, the law and research. John sits on the Adoption Leadership Board and the DfE's Advisory Group on Adoption Support. He was awarded an OBE in the New Year's Honours list 2015.

Jon Fayle has worked as a social worker or social work manager for most of his working life. He has also worked as a senior policy officer for the Youth Justice Board, mainly in the area of youth custody.

Jon is now a practising Independent Reviewing Officer (IRO). He helped to set up the National Association of Independent Reviewing Officers (NAIRO), with a view to enhancing the influence of the reviewing process for the benefit of children in care. He is now Vice Chair of NAIRO. Jon is Chair of the Board of Trustees of TACT, the fostering and adoption charity. Jon also works as a consultant and trainer in the area of IRO practice and policy, and fostering.

Yvonne Smith is married with one adult birth child. She has a background in working with vulnerable children and has been a foster carer for several years. Her own upbringing and raising her child has shaped the care and nurture that her family provides to their foster children. Yvonne has travelled to many interesting and beautiful places, however lives a few miles away from the place where she was born and raised in the midst of her family. She believes home really is where the heart is.

Annie (Surviving Safeguarding) writes a blog that aims to inform, support and advise all of those involved in the UK Child Protection Process from the unique perspective of a parent who has experienced, negotiated and survived. http://survivingsafeguarding.co.uk – A parent's guide to the child protection process.

Case Study Contributors

Case studies provided by:

Colin and Shona Marshall
Gabriella Mitchell
Jill Priddy
Leanne and Nathan Gale
Lian Platts
Marian Gardener
Mary and Paul Bakker
Paul Bakker
Ronda Cameron
Roseanne Phillips
Sandra Erdogan
Wendy Jordan
Zoe Axford